Teaching English Using ICT

A practical guide for secondary school teachers

Tom Rank, Chris Warren and Trevor Millum

continuum

Continuum International Publishing Group

The Tower Building
11 York Road
London SE1 7NX

80 Maiden Lane
Suite 704
New York, NY 10038

www.continuumbooks.com

British Library Cataloguing-in-Publication Data
A catalogue record for this book is available from the British Library.

ISBN: 978-1-4411-1782-3 (paperback)

Library of Congress Cataloging-in-Publication Data
Rank, Tom.
Teaching English using ICT : a practical guide for secondary school
teachers/
Tom Rank, Chris Warren, and Trevor Millum.
    p. cm.
Includes index.
ISBN 978-1-4411-1782-3 (alk. paper)
1. English language–Study and teaching (Secondary)–Computer-
assisted instruction. 2. English literature–Study and teaching
(Secondary)–Computer-assisted instruction. 3. Word processing in
education. 4. Information technology. I. Warren, Chris, 1953– II.
Millum, Trevor. III. Title.

LB1631.3.R36 2011
428.0071'2–dc22
                                                2010042892

Typeset by Newgen Imaging Systems Pvt Ltd, Chennai, India
Printed and bound in India

Contents

Acknowledgements

We should like to pay tribute to our colleagues in the National Association for the Teaching of English, particularly fellow members of the ICT Committee. We should also like to thank those who have contributed to the NATE projects that are mentioned in this book and who allowed us the privilege of visiting their classrooms. We are also grateful for the support of Richard Hammond of Becta on those projects to promote the practical use of ICT in the classroom. Especial thanks are due to Garry Pratt of Teachit for permission to use material previously published online on the service – the transformation section – and thanks too for the use of screenshots illustrating the *Wordwhiz* program.

We should also acknowledge the role of Creative Partnerships, whose support for creative practitioners in schools in the UK has enabled some really innovative work to take place; in particular Scunthorpe Church of England Primary School and practitioners Chris Webster and Jon Robson.

Introduction

ICT is now widely used in the teaching and learning of English, as it is in all areas of the curriculum. However, as most English teachers would acknowledge, there is still much more to do to make effective and enjoyable use of the technology. It is the purpose of this book to provide a very diverse set of inspirations and starting points so that we can make full use of this considerable potential.

The writers of this book are not technical wizards and have no wish to become such. We are experienced teachers of English and lovers of language and literature. In our view, English always comes first and technology of any kind, from the old overhead projector or spirit duplicator to the latest digital device or Web 2.0 application, must serve the teaching of the subject. It should serve the subject not by offering alternatives for the sake of it but because new technologies can extend, enhance or make more efficient what they already strive to achieve.

The structure of this book is based on the document called 'The Entitlement to ICT in Secondary English' produced by the National Association for the Teaching of English (NATE) with other key partners. Often referred to as 'the Entitlement Document', it was first published by Becta, at that time the government agency for ICT in education in England and Wales, in 2003. It provides an extremely elegant summary of the range of potentials represented by ICT and the way they map onto the teaching of English. As analysis of the relationship between the subject and technology, it hasn't been beaten, and we would recommend all English departments to obtain a copy. The current version can be found on the NATE site (www.nate.org.uk/page/ict_policy). This is perhaps also the place to explain, for non-UK readers, our use of the abbreviation 'ICT'. It stands for information and communication technology and has been adopted in schools and colleges in place of 'IT' to signify the part played by a wide range of technology, not merely to process information but also (crucially for education) for communication. It also indicates a much wider remit than computers at a time when most students carry around at least one mobile device more powerful and versatile than the machines that first started to appear in classrooms 30 years ago.

We see the development of ICT in English as a progression, a gradual evolution, rather than a dramatic leap into the unknown. It's a bit like rungs on a ladder – each rung needs to be in place for ascent to be safe, and it's risky to skip a rung, and dangerous to leave one out. In the chapters that follow, you will find activities which are well within the capabilities (or the availability of resources) of those who are beginning to use ICT in their teaching. There will also be ideas to extend and build upon such practice and there will be suggestions which will appeal to those who are already confident ICT users.

We all know in theory about the fluidity, the slipperiness and flexibility of language, and we experience it when we talk. Traditional methods of recording language – typically writing with a pen and ink – tend to lock words in place, fix their form, sequence and impact. The computer, by contrast, accentuates the fluidity of language. It enables experiment and constant readjustment. Not only can the position and form of individual words be altered, a writer can also radically change the visual impact of the text by selecting different fonts, sizes, and layouts.

ICT also allows us to move beyond words on the page or the screen to embrace other modes of communication. Images, still and moving, together with audio recording and editing can be employed in ways which are both innovative and more manageable. Furthermore, we can exploit the still developing world of Web 2.0 applications to the advantage of our students and their learning without ever losing sight of our overriding purpose – developing our best practice in the teaching of English.

In the following chapters, we also try to counteract the impoverishing effect of simple wrong/right activities – the black-or-white, tick-or-cross common to many computer lessons. English teachers need to stand against these designs, however useful they might be in other subject areas. Our subject is character-ized for the most part by shades of meaning, by full-spectrum colours, and by deliberate departure from established rules. To sum up, computers applied narrowly can restrict and box us in; we find ourselves cabined, cribbed, confined. Used imaginatively they can make us as broad and general as the casing air!

This brings us to another of the aspects we would like to most emphasize: that of collaboration. Ever since computers first appeared in English classrooms, collaboration has been one of the special contributions of technology to our subject. This book aims to inspire you to investigate and exploit forms of co-operation uniquely enabled by communications technology.

Many of the lesson suggestions place an emphasis on flexibility and experiment. The outcome of this approach is that teachers and pupils need to engage, need to debate, discuss, disagree and argue. The experimental approach isn't neat, silent, solitary, pre-ordained and fixed of outcome. It is sometimes noisy, always enjoyable, exciting, messy, engaging, fascinating, frequently obsessive, and you cannot always be completely certain of the final result. But it can lead to the most exciting lessons you will teach.

A case in point – poetry

To make a case for the use of ICT in English we might look at one aspect of the subject, poetry (the NATE 'Hard To Teach' project that we mention several times in this book found this area an especially difficult one to communicate in class). If we ask 'how might the use of ICT enhance or extend the enjoyment of poetry?' the answers illustrate very well the methodology, purpose and spirit of this book. We start by identifying the unique qualities of poetry and then we match them with the special attributes of ICT.

What is poetry?

- Poetry is an art form composed from words
- Poetry is by its nature playful
- Poetry is multimedia by nature
- Poetry is rule-bound
- Poetry has a ritual and highly significant function in society

So how does ICT interact with and support these qualities of poetry?

- ICT adds fluidity to words
- This playfulness can extend to include the physical arrangement of words on the page, which can be experimented with painlessly on a computer
- ICT allows poems to broken down and rebuilt
- ICT enables multimedia approaches to poetry
- ICT allows poets to publish their work to worldwide audiences

Let's look at these attributes in turn:

Poetry can be described as an art form composed of words, based on the sound and rhythm of words arranged in lines, and the emotional and pictorial power these compressed expressions have to communicate feelings, thought, belief, philosophy and sense information to the mind of the audience. Poetry is by its nature playful; both in the way that words are organized and the way meanings are juxtaposed. Even a poem's layout out on the page can be an excuse for wit or powerful dramatic effect.

ICT enables playfulness with text; it adds fluidity to words, encouraging a spirit of risk-free experimentation – words can be moved around, they can be changed, they can be deleted and added to in powerfully efficient ways impossible before. ICT will not only allow this high-level form of editing, it will also enable the writer to choose the final font for the publication of the poem – a function that used to be the exclusive province of a compositor or printer. Computers have therefore added immensely to the sense of control over the shaping and the final form of a composition.

What is lost in the process? Much has been written (Daniel Chandler launched this debate several years ago) about the way ICT detracts from the human, 'touchy-feeliness' of the handwritten artefact, its messiness, its crossings-out and hard-mapped insertions, its arrows and jotted marginalia, its unmistakeable encapsulation of an individual's unique mood and personality. Looking at the drafts fortuitously left behind by Wilfred Owen you can see the point. If he'd had a laptop at the front (weird image!), what a world of thought and expression would have been lost in the clinical up-to-datedness of the digital draft!

If one wishes to preserve a thought-map of a composition one has to take special steps to do so – switch on track-changes, save regular drafts, make frequent printouts. However, nothing really matches the scruffy handwritten versions for power. Most writers operate some sort of mixed economy – some composition and editing on screen, some handwritten edits on printouts. Both forms should be celebrated and their special advantages acknowledged. It is vital that teachers don't weigh in strongly on either side. For some students, handwriting is a source of immense pride, a place where personality and flair find expression. For such students, computers can seem to rob them of something vital. For others, handwriting is a private shame and an embarrassment: computers offer liberation and new motivations. Creative, joyful coexistence of ICT and traditional drafting forms should be the rule – not some mutually exclusive regime.

Playfulness with words (and by this we do not want to imply any lack of serious intent) can be extended to include the physical arrangement of words on the page – the witty recognitions of concrete poetry or careful indentations that convey formal meanings can be experimented with painlessly on a computer.

ICT has a related part to play in the *reading* of poetry. Teachers can disturb the order of lines (de-sequencing), or collapse a text to provide completely new ICT-generated pre-reading activities. ICT allows poems to broken down and rebuilt so that new ways of reading the text can be explored. Typically, lines can be re-sequenced without the aid of scissors. Rhyme-schemes and other formal features can be mapped. A puzzle element can provide a hook, and ICT makes such puzzles practical to construct.

No one watching students working with the Developing Tray software can ever quite forget the moments of revelation, the dawning of comprehension as shadowed meanings begin to light up through thought and discussion. Something magical happens if you stay with text, if you chew on it for more than the usual half-distracted three minutes. As long as we don't as teachers blight the memory of the writing with some pre-digested, regurgitated version of its meaning, students begin to discover layers of meaning, personal resonances and hidden nuances. The problem has always been to find a way to keep attention fixed long enough for the text to cast its own spell (and there's more on Developing Tray in Chapter 9).

Text Mapping, invented by Tony Clifford, remains a particularly brilliant use of the word processor. As a reading/analysis approach, it relies on the fact that a word processor can mark a text using font, style, font size, colour and effects such as highlighting. All of these features can co-locate on the same word without rendering it illegible.

Each feature can be assigned a meaning by students, and the key to the map written at the foot of the page. The lesson concludes with full presentations from each group doing the mapping, explaining how they have marked the text, and discussing what they have discovered in the process. The fun of manipulating the mapping tools keeps concentration high; and the challenge of the final presentation ensures inventive, valuable critical thinking is achieved.

Poetry is multimedia by nature; it interacts with other art forms. Visual art (the poetry of Blake is a supreme example) has always been associated with poetry, and fine poetry paints word-pictures in the mind. Poetry, because of its origins and its strong rhythmic basis, is directly related to music and song.

The words 'lyric', (words set to be sung to the lyre) and 'ballad' attest to this relationship. Drama was written in poetry for centuries and indeed, some of the greatest plays in existence are written entirely in verse, while poetry in song-making pervades every corner of our lives. Modern drama and modern film invariably include elements of song, occasionally direct use of poetry and in the ironic or metaphorical deployment of images and poetic effects.

ICT enables multimedia approaches to poetry, the combination of words with images, with movies – cartoons and films. It facilitates composition of music and makes arranging images in special sequences an easy task. It also helps with the final production or presentation.

The key thing to remember is not to take the ICT at face value – it will do what you want it to, though perhaps it was actually designed for a narrow, non-educational context. A classic example of this aspect of ICT is a program like Microsoft PowerPoint. Everything about PowerPoint says it is there to help adults in a commercial setting to communicate with other adults. The way the program works, the way it generates bullet-points, the background designs you are offered by default – all these betray its sales/commercial origins. However, it can be made to work in other ways if you have a clear sense of your intentions. The irritatingly predictable bullet-points can be subverted, given new life and purpose by underscoring or counterpointing a live spoken performance. What's displayed on the screen can be in ironic contrast to the words. Wonderful examples of this approach exist; where images are shown to go with a poem and don't just plod along slavishly replicating the obvious. They can be ironic, deflationary, shocking, metaphorical, funny and tragic. Individual words from the poem, or new words chosen for impact, can be blown up to fill the entire screen – often to stunning effect. In this way Power-Point can be used in a patterned series of symmetrical or asymmetrical words and images to match the rhythm and structure of the poem.

The thinking and planning behind such a project is by its nature rich in literary and learning potential. There is no shortage of pictures either – images abound both on disk and on the internet; they can also be captured to order using digital cameras. A project that embodies these sorts of approaches is more likely to engage and motivate – students are put in the position of creative participation as opposed to passive consumption. It's always better to learn by doing.

Poetry is rule-bound (though, of course, some poets break the rules), has formal and informal structures, is organized in special ways.

ICT offers a useful range of techniques for analysing the underlying rules of verse, allowing students to investigate the patterns in a piece of writing. New approaches are being invented all the time. Examples include the special fridge-magnets designed to explore the structure of sonnets, techniques developed to give students insights into deep structures in a poem. Other tools allow clever annotation so that a class can work as a group on analysis. Text Mapping, discussed here and in Chapter 3, makes patterned features visually and graphically apparent – an excellent method which appeals to a range of learning styles.

What these ideas have in common is a startling realization that ICT can scramble and unscramble a piece of writing, can select and isolate special elements in it, can allow activities that are simply impossible without the computer's help.

The thought occurs that there may be new rules and new forms of writing enabled uniquely by ICT.

- Choose your own adventure? Why not choose your own poem?
- Static words on the page? Why not animate the text? (I recall Chandler's experimental programs for the BBC Model B computer!)
- One form of text? Why not exploit the power of hypertext for new forms?
- Solitary poets? Why not bring writers together in new ways for collaborative composition? What we call a 'wiki'.
- Remote and semi-deified poet-people? Why not connect established writers and young enthusiastic pupils into collaborative creative communities?

Most of what is listed here has been tried before somewhere or other, with usually enormous success. So why can't we have more of it? ICT has opened the door for us – all we have to do is walk through it.

Poetry has a ritual and highly significant function in society. It was the first verbal art form, the first channel chosen by our ancestors to capture and transmit history and culture. It is no accident that hymns are sung, that greeting cards carry verses, that we have a poet laureate to punctuate state events with pithy compositions or that we use powerfully persuasive verses to sell things.

The internet allows writers to publish their work to worldwide audiences in a matter of seconds. It has encouraged the growth of internet poetry-writing circles all over the world. The concept of society as defined by geographical constraints, village or town, county or state, or even the borders of a nation, no longer adequately describes what is happening. The internet has made us part of a world society.

Children in school join such a community. What they publish on the internet can be read by someone on the other side of the planet.

A primary school head reported how two of his pupils were transformed by receiving feedback from America. They had published poems on a children's site and a kindly American professor had written to them with words of encouragement. The effect was dramatic, both on their motivation, self-esteem and future work. He called it a 'trigger moment' and we know what he means; we've seen moments like it ourselves – they are precious for every classroom teacher. The lesson is that we need to embrace the new global opportunities offered by the internet. We shouldn't just watch children in Africa on television – let's establish creative contact with them via email and celebrate each other's writing and experience. The opportunity is there, and the common, world-embracing art form of poetry gives us a common language, a common project and a common goal.

Organization of the book

We wish this book to have as wide an application as possible. With this in mind, we have tried to avoid references to particular curricula, examinations or other nomenclature which tie us down to a specific place or a restricting purpose. As a result, the book is organized according to those kinds of things which *all* teachers of English will want their students to experience.

In **Using ICT to Explore and Investigate,** we demonstrate how ICT can be used to help students discover things about a text (of whatever kind) which would be difficult or impossible to achieve by other means. In **Using ICT to Analyse Language,** we take a look at the powerful tools offered by Corpus approaches and Wordle for taking that discovery to the next stage.

In **Using ICT to Respond, Interpret, Reflect and Evaluate,** we show how students can express their reactions to and interpretations of texts in creative and engaging ways.

Using ICT to Compose and Create offers ideas to assist students in express-ing themselves. However else it may be used in other subjects, in English ICT is a tool for creativity. Within **Using ICT to Transform** you will find teaching approaches which enable students to understand the conventions of different genres and text types and to see the impact of often subtle alterations to language, with a range of writing activities enabled by the technology to take existing text and transform it.

In **Using ICT to Present and Perform** teachers will find examples of the many ways in which ICT can be employed to share students' work and to enhance not just their reading and writing but their speaking and listening also.

ICT allows, indeed encourages us, to communicate and collaborate. **Using ICT to Communicate and Collaborate is** a chapter which explores the ways in which this facility can be used most purposefully in English.

Clearly many of the approaches described in the preceding chapters will have contributed to inspire and engage students, but the chapter **Using ICT to Inspire and Engage,** focuses on programs designed specifically to spark the imagination and motivate students to discuss and write.

A chapter on **Using ICT to Entertain** might surprise readers, but who has not wanted to enliven mundane or repetitive tasks? Here are ways to do so.

We shan't be providing detailed instructions for using particular software and hardware. Applications and equipment are developing all the time and there are a variety of systems installed in schools, each with different features. Having said that, we do include some details of ideas we've found useful both here and (in more depth) on the accompanying Continuum website (http://education.rank.continuumbooks.com). Good software should be easy to use – and if you are stuck, our best advice is either to find a colleague who can help or involve your students in exploring a new ICT tool. Learning together is one of the best methods and between you may well come up with unexpected ways of exploiting the technology's potential. This has certainly been our experience and that of the teachers whose work we feature in this book.

Enjoy the journey!

Where you see this icon, you can find online versions of the text for down- load or for projecting onto your interactive whiteboard, or additional materi- als on the companion website. Please go to http://education.rank. continuumbooks.com to access these resources. You will also find useful web links, further reading and a glossary on the companion website.

1

Using ICT to Explore and Investigate

It is a natural desire of the English teacher to want students to explore texts and to help them in doing so. Although there is a crucial and too often neglected place in every classroom for reading – or listening or viewing – a text for its own simple pleasure, we know that there is, equally often, a desire or a need to look more closely: to explore, to investigate – to look beneath the surface.

'Explore' and 'investigate' are terms so close to each other such that they are sometimes indistinguishable, but the distinction is worth bearing in mind. When we, as teachers, want students to **explore** a text, we are not setting a specific task. We are hoping that in their exploration they will discover things of interest in the same way that an explorer may discover a lake or a mountain – or merely an unusual species of goat. When we ask them to **investigate**, we have something more precise in mind: there is more of the detective about it, than the explorer. The student, indeed, may be looking for clues, for evidence.

There are two dangers in trying to assist the student in these areas. One is the temptation to give too much information, to dictate notes or give handouts or simply to tell them too much. In this way there is no room for students to form their own opinions or to come up with something fresh (or something which is fresh to them). Another aspect of this is the immediate reference to websites or publishers' 'Notes' or 'Guides'. There is a place for these – but much later in the process.

The other danger lies in the list of comprehension questions, for example, 'What does the writer imply by the word "scuttled" in line 7?' or 'What words does the poet use to describe the tramp in verse one?', questions which can be answered without much thought and no involvement. Some questions, of course, are valuable and can lead the student in useful directions. 'To what extent is this a negative or depressing description?' or 'What is your reaction to the ending of this chapter?' are the kinds of questions which throw the ball back into the student's court rather than expecting them to land it in the precise square you have marked out on your side of the net. Other ways of helping the student into a text are described below and you will find still more throughout this book, especially in Chapter 5 'Using ICT to Transform'.

How can ICT help in exploration and investigation?

This chapter will look at a variety of ways in which ICT can be employed, some of which are very simple indeed and all of which offer ways into a text which would be hard (and sometimes impossible) to achieve by traditional means. Along the way we will look at ways of investigating written texts, still images and spoken texts. It will also consider how interactive (Web 2.0) technologies can assist students in collaborative investigations.

Exploring and investigating written texts

Sequencing

One simple and popular means of investigating a text is to de-sequence it and ask students to re-sequence it. Anyone who has undertaken this using small pieces of paper or card will understand the disadvantages. As well as inconveniences during and after a lesson, this activity requires a fair amount of preparation. Using ICT, we can minimize preparation and do away with the most common in-class difficulties.

Taking a poem as an example, we can create an almost instant lesson once we have the text in electronic format.

Twinkle twinkle little star
How I wonder what you are
Up above the world so high
Like a diamond in the sky

becomes:

How I wonder what you are
Like a diamond in the sky
Up above the world so high
Twinkle twinkle little star

Once this is projected onto a screen (interactive or not) you have a lesson – a learning opportunity! In order to put a text of any kind back into its original sequence, a student has to get to grips with it. It cannot be done without engaging the brain. Almost all texts have a sequence, an order or direction to them. The exceptions would include descriptions where it really doesn't matter whether one item is described before another, certain lists, perhaps some persuasive texts. There will be some poems which fall into this category too. Most texts, however, have an order, whether it be narrative or chronological development, a logical order of instructions or directions, a build up of rhetoric or simply one arrangement which reads better than others.

Even in instances where the order of a text is not obvious or necessary, there is scope for de- and re-sequencing in order to discover which possibilities students can find. In a poem such as 'The Hollow Men' by T. S. Eliot there might be any number of interpretations, all of them worthy of discussion and of comparison with the original.

Try this

This is an activity which can be carried out as a whole class or by individuals/ pairs working at their own computers. In the whole class situation, it is a good idea to provide students with a printed version which they can look at for five or ten minutes, perhaps with a partner, so that when the class discussion begins everyone is prepared.

Whichever way the activity is organized, it is worth experimenting with different ways of reordering the lines. Interactive whiteboard software will usually include a facility to drag items around the screen, and these can comprise pieces of text. PowerPoint in Edit mode can be used in a similar way. However, the simplest method is to use a word processor. In Word, you (or your students) can cut and paste, drag and drop or use Shift, Alt and cursors to move lines. Of course, ICT encourages trial and error, a most powerful tool for learners.

Making use of the *Sort* function in Word

A text can be rapidly de-sequenced in Word by using the alphabetical *Sort* function. This will sort and arrange a text in order of the initial letter of each line. For example, Shakespeare's Sonnet 18:

> And every fair from fair sometime declines,
> And often is his gold complexion dimmed;
> And summer's lease hath all too short a date.
> But thy eternal summer shall not fade
> By chance, or nature's changing course untrimmed.
> Nor lose possession of that fair thou ow'st;
> Nor shall death brag thou wand'rest in his shade,
> Rough winds do shake the darling buds of May,
> Shall I compare thee to a summer's day?
> So long as men can breathe or eyes can see,
> So long lives this, and this gives life to thee
> Sometime too hot the eye of heaven shines,
> Thou art more lovely and more temperate.
> When in eternal lines to time thou grow'st,

It will work in a similar way with prose, sorting paragraphs rather than lines. If you wish to de-sequence within a paragraph using this method, you will have to insert line breaks manually using the Enter key.

A sequencing activity encourages students to look out for markers such as 'In the first place . . .', 'However . . .' 'Later . . .' or rhyme words in the case of sonnets or other rhyming poetry. It can also be used as a way of investigating plays as this example from 'Romeo and Juliet' will show, the order of the speeches having been altered:

> **Juliet**   Then have my lips the sin that they have took.
> **Romeo**   Have not saints lips, and holy palmers too?
> **Romeo**   O then, dear saint, let lips do what hands do:
>   They pray. Grant thou, lest faith turn to despair.
> **Romeo**   [Approaching JULIET.]
>   If I profane with my unworthiest hand
>   This holy shrine, the gentle sin is this:
>   My lips, two blushing pilgrims, ready stand
>   To smooth that rough touch with a tender kiss.
> **Juliet**   Saints do not move, though grant for prayer's sake.
> **Juliet**   Ay, pilgrim, lips that they must use in prayer.
> **Romeo**   Sin from my lips? O trespass sweetly urged!
>   Give me my sin again.

Juliet	Good pilgrim, you do wrong your hand too much,
	Which mannerly devotion shows in this;
	For saints have hands that pilgrims' hands do touch,
	And palm to palm is holy palmers' kiss.
Romeo	Then move not while my prayer's effect I take.
	[Kisses her.]
	Thus from my lips, by thine my sin is purged.

Do not underestimate the difficulty of this kind of activity. In fact – try it yourself first! An even harder version would be to de-sequence the lines within individual speeches, for example:

[Kisses her.]
And palm to palm is holy palmers' kiss.
For saints have hands that pilgrims' hands do touch,
Give me my sin again.
If I profane with my unworthiest hand

Juliet	Ay, pilgrim, lips that they must use in prayer.
Juliet	Good pilgrim, you do wrong your hand too much,
Juliet	Saints do not move, though grant for prayer's sake.
Juliet	Then have my lips the sin that they have took.
	My lips, two blushing pilgrims, ready stand
Romeo	[Approaching JULIET.]
Romeo	Have not saints lips, and holy palmers too?
Romeo	O then, dear saint, let lips do what hands do:
Romeo	Sin from my lips? O trespass sweetly urged!
Romeo	Then move not while my prayer's effect I take.
	They pray. Grant thou, lest faith turn to despair.
	This holy shrine, the gentle sin is this:
	Thus from my lips, by thine my sin is purged.
	To smooth that rough touch with a tender kiss.
	Which mannerly devotion shows in this;

Hidden words

Curiosity is a powerful motivator; puzzles are more popular than problems; quizzes more so than tests. ICT allows these factors to be utilized for pedagogical purposes in innovative ways. For example, what would be more engaging, a text where you could see every word (and perhaps be immediately turned off or discouraged) or one which hid its nature from you until you revealed it?

Interactive whiteboard software has features which allow you to hide parts of whatever is displayed, be it text or image. Such features as the *spotlight* (showing only whatever you 'shine' the spotlight on) or the *blinds* (hiding sections of the screen from top, bottom or side) can be used in this way.

There are also commercial software applications such as Developing Tray™ which add functionality such as the option to reveal certain letters or to reward correct choices with points (or deduct them when help is requested). These are worth investigating.

Alternatively, mystery texts can be created with your word processor by making all or some of the words disappear:

> The   , then as now, are kitchen   which do not sit neatly and demurely on one side of the house as a European herb   might, but encircle it with some abandon.   often disappear entirely within their verdant, forest-like   . Black pepper vines clamber tenaciously up mango   , the peppercorns huddling together in bright green clusters like bunches of embryo grapes. Nutmeg fruit hang like tennis balls, ready to split open and offer both their nuts and their special bonus, curls of tangerine-coloured mace. Cinnamon, clove and tamarind   compete for a view of the sky while cardamom stays close to the ground, hugging its mother   . There are ginger and turmeric plants as well, sending fingers of their tubers into the cool dark   . Above all, there are the two   that give the foods of Kerala their special character – the sweetly aromatic curry leaf   and the arching, swaying coconut palm.

Unlike cloze passages (where words are omitted from the text) these words can be made to reappear at will, simply by double-clicking on them and changing the font colour to black (or any other colour). As you may have guessed, the blanks in the passage have been created by changing their colour to white. If you wish to be different, change your background colour (i.e. the colour of your 'paper') to any colour you think appropriate and then make your hidden words the same colour.

A completely hidden mystery text is, in many ways, more interesting and offers more opportunities for language work or literary investigation than a partially or largely revealed one. Take an interesting text and alter all of the writing to the same colour as the background. Project it for the class to see and, to begin with, reveal words at random. (A double-click within the text will select a single word which you can then colour and make visible.) Pupils can come up to the board, or use a wireless mouse to achieve the same effect. Once you have several words revealed, pupils can begin to make deductions and predictions: they can truly explore an unknown text-land. Or it could be seen in terms of an archaeological investigation: digging up words and trying to make connections between them.

To what purpose are we excavating? Perhaps to become reacquainted with a previously seen text, possibly as a revision activity. Perhaps to investigate syntax through a very close look at the structure of sentences. Perhaps to identify a text type. (If you don't wish to become enmired in nitpicking definitions of these, simply pose the question: 'What kind of text is this? What can we say about it at an early stage? To what extent are our earlier predictions modified in the light of subsequent revelations?')

A more sophisticated mystery text can be created by making an interactive word wall. This can be done using Word and the instructions are provided online.

Alphabetical texts

Another way in which texts can be investigated in an unusual and thought-provoking manner is to decontextualize the words. This is sometimes known as 'collapsing' a text, alphabeticizing it or simply creating 'fridge magnets'. The result of the process is the same: the pupil is presented with all the words of a given text arranged in alphabetical order. See the examples which follow.

These words can be used simply and effectively as a way of inspiring creative writing – of which more elsewhere. Here we are focusing on collapsing a text in order to discover more about it. Seeing a text from an unusual angle can reveal things about it which even the most familiar reader may not have noticed. To take as an example two poems with which I thought I was familiar – John Clare's sonnet 'I love to see the summer beaming forth' and John Keats' 'To Autumn':

a about again and and and and and and beaming beetles
blobs bright bright bull clear clear clouds clumps come day
deep drain flag floating floods flower flowers forth from
gold grass half happy hay head hen her her hiding I I I I in
in insects its lake lake leaning like like lilies love love love
mare meadow meadow moor nest north o'er on place play
pushes reed rushes rustle sack sailing see see see seeks
shook shore sport stain stand summer summer swings that
the the the the the the the the the the the the the to to to to to to
upon water way when where where white whiten wild
willow wind winds wings with wood wool

Seen in its collapsed form, Clare's sonnet immediately throws up obvious repetitions: the use of the first person, the use of love and like, for example. Is this typical of a Romantic poet, writing about nature? Let's compare the same number of lines from Keats and see what we find:

a abroad all amid and and and and and apples bees bend bless
bosom-friend budding by cease cells clammy close
conspiring core cottage-trees days fill find flowers for for
fruit fruit fruitfulness gourd hair has hath hazel him how
kernel later load maturing may mellow mists more more

moss'd never not o'er-brimm'd of of oft plump ripeness
round run season seeks seen set shells soft-lifted sometimes
still store summer sun sweet swell that thatch-eves the the
the the the the the the the the thee their they think thy thy to to
to to to until vines warm who whoever will wind winnowing
with with with with with

What we might find are two very different Romantic poets. One whose involvement with nature is extremely personal and the other who observes in as much, if not more detail, but keeps himself at a distance, like a Constable depicting the landscape.

We might notice other things: the repetition of those little words we tend to overlook: to, with, the. These are important words in 'To Autumn'. The first stanza is driven by these words. The season and the sun are conspiring **with** each other **to** do a whole list of specific things – hence the word 'the', not 'a'. This is not a generalized view, this is a view which sees and celebrates exact concrete things; **the** hazel shell, not **a** hazel shell or even 'hazel shells'. How else would we have noticed this?

Continuing to look through the poem we would see that 'with' continues to feature, that 'the' and 'a' are equally represented in the second stanza but that in the final stanza, 'the' is dominant again. This forensic kind of investigation may not be to every student's taste but it may well appeal to those who thought literature and especially poetry was the domain of the vague and subjective response.

As well as looking closely at literature the collapsed text approach can be used to make the examination of text types develop from a sterile application of rules to an interactive engagement.

What do we notice about this text?

17th a a a a a a a a a also an and and and and are at
attractive banquettes bar beaten been below black
brass bronze built-in button-back century chairs
chimney-piece coal coal colours comfortable corner
curving decorated end feel finish fire fire great gun-
dog hand has has have horse-race houses in inglenook
inn into is it its lamp left lived-in lively low
mantlepiece modern must now of of of of of of of on
on once one one part plush print problematic red right
room shiny small small snug soft spindleback sporting
statuette tables taking The the the the the the the them
there this three two-roomed up village wall warm
watercolour what white whole with wooden

The first thing we might notice if we try to create our own piece of writing using these words is the lack of pronouns. No one could construct a narrative from this selection. Another thing is the dominance of nouns and adjectives. It's true that out of context a verb is hard to tell from a noun and from an adjective. That in itself can lead to a useful activity (see later in this chapter). However, even on a very rough count we can guess that nouns and adjectives well outnumber verbs. What kind of writing lends itself to this balance?

The answer is a certain kind of descriptive writing where space is at a premium and every word must count. Hence a high ratio of adjectives to nouns, which in other forms of writing would strike the reader as clumsy and overdone. This is the world of guides and brochures, where each unit has a severely limited word count. In the case of the example given earlier: *The Good Pub Guide.*

Categorizing by word classes is usually a sterile activity, but if you introduce an element of allowable ambiguity and some kinetic reward, it can be more interesting. Take the above example text and create a table beneath it. Allow the same word to be placed into more than one category. Ask students to colour such words. In the example we have used bold, italic and underline:

Nouns	Adjectives	Verbs
banquettes	attractive	beaten
bar	black	<u>colours</u>
chimney-piece	brass	**curving**
chairs	bronze	
coal	built-in	
<u>colours</u>	button-back	
corner	seventeenth century	
	coal	
	comfortable	
	corner	
	curving	

Of course, you know that chairs could be a verb and brass a noun, but we are not trying to be pedantic, just to offer choice and to see that even when ambiguity has been taken into account this passage is dominated by adjectives and nouns. This will be an opportunity to send students on a research task to find other examples of such texts (e.g. holiday brochures, estate agent descriptions, bird-watchers' guides etc.) and then examine them to see if they share the same characteristics.

Try the collapsed text technique on any piece of writing you are interested in. It's easy to do as long as you have an electronic copy of the words. Anything from a whole Shakespeare play to the speeches of Lincoln, Martin Luther King and Barack Obama can be looked at in this way with outcomes which may simply reinforce what you expected or surprise you with new insights.

Searching

Whichever word processor you have access to, it can be used to investigate texts in even more precise ways. One of the most useful of these is the ability to search, find and mark a particular word. This might be 'blood' in *Macbeth*, or 'love' in *Romeo and Juliet*. Equally, you might want to search for 'blood' in *Romeo and Juliet* and 'love' in *Macbeth*: the results might surprise. In fact, this facility allows ordinary students rather than university professors to carry out innovative wide ranging research which is genuinely experimental. Is it true that 'blood' and 'bloody' occur more in *Macbeth* than in other plays? How does Shakespeare use 'thee', 'thou' and 'thy' compared to 'you' and 'your'? How frequently do certain characters meet in a Dickens novel? And so on.

The underlying technique in all these investigations employs the Find and Replace function in conjunction with the Highlight tool (or any of the emphases which can be applied to fonts such as colour, bold, italic and underline). A typical Find/Replace dialogue box will provide the option of searching for a word or a phrase and marking it in one of those ways. More detailed instructions can be found online. You can, of course, search much shorter texts and mark them equally interestingly. Keats' 'To Autumn', which we looked at earlier, could be investigated in this way, marking the word 'with', say, in bold:

> Season of mists and mellow fruitfulness,
> Close bosom-friend of the maturing sun;
> Conspiring **with** him how to load and bless
> **With** fruit the vines that round the thatch-eves run;
> To bend **with** apples the moss'd cottage-trees,
> And fill all fruit **with** ripeness to the core;
> To swell the gourd, and plump the hazel shells
> **With** a sweet kernel; to set budding more,
> And still more, later flowers for the bees,
> Until they think warm days will never cease,
> For summer has o'er-brimmed their clammy cells.

And while I wouldn't recommend alliteration spotting for its own sake, it can be fun to do a search for certain sounds and colour them in different colours. Here you will have to be satisfied with black and white but you can examine it in full colour on the Continuum site:

> Glory be to God **f**or dappled thing₅ --
> For ₅ᵏie₅ of ᶜouple-ᶜolour a₅ a brinded ᶜow;
> For ro₅e-mole₅ all in ₅tipple upon trout that ₅wim;

Freₛh-fireᶜoal ᶜheₛtnut-fallₛ; finᶜheₛ' wingₛ;
Landₛᶜape plotted and pieᶜed – fold, **f**allow, and plough;
And all tradeₛ, their gear and taᶜᵏle and trim.
All thingₛ ᶜounter, original, ₛpare, ₛtrange;
Whatever iₛ fiᶜᵏle, freᶜᵏled, (who ᵏnowₛ how?)
With ₛwift, ₛlow; ₛweet, ₛour; adazzle, dim;
He **f**atherₛ-forth whoₛe beauty iₛ paₛt ᶜhange:
Praiₛe him.

As you can see in this example (G. M. Hopkins' 'Pied Beauty'), much can be achieved with bold, superscript and subscript to bring out repetitions of certain letters. As with any word-spotting (so similar to bird-spotting) activity, the crucial aspect is to be able to say why such and such an effect has been used by the writer. If, as here, you can't think of any reason except sheer joy and pleasure in the sounds of words, say so!

The analysis of Shakespeare's use of thee and thou requires a small adjustment to this technique. Imagine you are going to look at the way in which Beatrice and Benedick interact in Act IV of *Much Ado About Nothing*. You want to see how Shakespeare uses the familiar thee, thou, thy and thine. To do this you will need to compare it with his use of you, your and yours. As mentioned earlier, you will need to search the text for each of the first set (remember to check 'whole words only' or 'thou' will throw up 'thought' etc.), marking them with, say, red. Then, change the highlight colour to, say, green, and search for you, your and yours. Scroll though the text until you find a place where the reds and greens intersect; this will be the interesting part.

Benedick: By my sword, Beatrice, *thou* lovest me.
Beatrice: Do not swear, and eat it.
Benedick: I will swear by it that **you** love me; and I will make him eat it that says I love not **you**.
Beatrice: Will **you** not eat **your** word?
Benedick: With no sauce that can be devised to it. I protest I love *thee*.
Beatrice: Why, then, God forgive me!
Benedick: What offence, sweet Beatrice?
Beatrice: **You** have stayed me in a happy hour: I was about to protest I loved **you**.
Benedick: And do it with all *thy* heart.
Beatrice: I love **you** with so much of my heart that none is left to protest.
Benedick: Come, bid me do any thing for *thee*.
Beatrice: Kill Claudio.

So here we can see (without the emphasis of colour) Benedick using *thee* and *thy* and Beatrice resisting: she sticks to **you** and **your**. Elsewhere in the play you will find it used slightly differently, as superiors address inferiors with the more familiar form.

Think how many other investigations you and your students can carry out using these techniques!

Exploring and investigating images

ICT does not just afford us opportunities to explore and investigate written texts. It enables us to explore visual communications and combinations of visual, audio and print:

- combinations of text and graphics in print, for example, newspaper or magazine pages; book covers
- pictures, for example, paintings; news photos
- *multimodal texts*, for example, websites; touch-screen guides
- moving images, for example, video clips; feature films

One or two of the techniques described in the preceding sections can be modified to apply to the first two of these. For further discussion of moving image and multimodal texts, see Chapter 6: Using ICT to Present and Perform.

Picture wall

Using a technique similar to that employed in mystery texts we can hide and reveal sections of a picture, a magazine page or a book cover, to take some obvious examples.

There may be a connection with a text we are studying (e.g. 'The Lady of Shallott' or photographs from the World War I trenches) or simply with a period with which we are concerned, such as the Victorian or Romantic. Alternatively, our objective may be to discover the nature of the text (audience, purpose, genre, period and so on) as we would with a written text.

Whatever the objective, the 'hiding and revealing' approach has the same purpose: to focus attention on specifics rather than to be distracted by a general impression.

The 'spotlight' and 'blinds' features of interactive whiteboard software, which were described earlier in this chapter, can be used for this purpose. When doing so, it is useful for the teacher to have a copy of the picture available for quick reference to enable the spotlight, for example, to be used effectively. We might want to show an emblem or symbol rather than a part of an image which is an immediate 'give away' (the flowers in Ophelia's hands rather than her face, for instance) or a sub-heading rather than a headline.

Another method which can be neatly organized and allows controlled student access involves using Word or a spreadsheet such as Excel. Both depend upon inserting a picture and then hiding it behind cells which are shaded to obscure the image. As Word is more likely to be familiar to readers of this book, we will describe that method. Create a Table in Word with cells of a reasonable size, say 2.5 cm squares. Select the whole table and then go to Table Properties and choose Borders and Shading. Choose a colour and apply it. In the example shown here, grey is the colour.

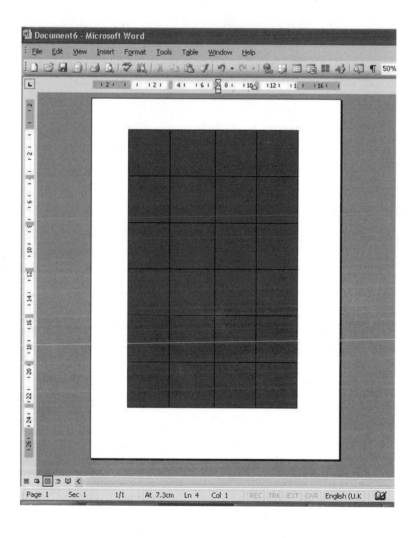

Now go to Format > Background and choose Printed Watermark. Select Picture Watermark and then use Select Picture to navigate to where you have saved the image you wish to use. Having selected it, uncheck Washout and then OK. (These instructions, together with another way of doing this, can be found on the Continuum website.) The picture will appear behind your table.

To reveal the picture behind that section, you will need to 'uncover' it. Rather than go to Table Properties and click through several dialogue boxes, make the Tables and Borders toolbar visible (View > Toolbars > Tables and toolbars). This will enable you to simply click on the Fill icon and select No Fill. Cells can then be uncovered in whichever order you wish .

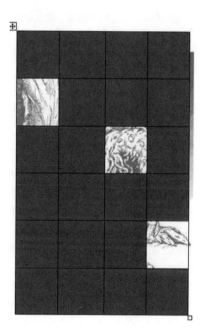

Alternatively, you can set up a macro to do the job with one key press. See the Continuum site for more details about hiding images and setting up macros.

Another useful feature, analogous to the annotation tool in interactive whiteboard software, is Insert Comment so that you or students can annotate the picture, attaching each note to a specific cell.

Comment [MSOffice1]: Factual text: nutrition information

Comment [MSOffice2]: Persuasive text

Exploring and investigating the spoken word

One area in which ICT is underused in the English classroom is that of sound. Whereas teachers were adept at managing reel-to-reel recorders and then cassette sound recorders, the recording and playing of sound seems to have receded into the background over the last few years. Paradoxically, sound recording is easier than ever and no one has to manage awkward tapes or cassettes anymore.

There are a number of hand-held voice recorders on the market, basically microphones which store your recordings on a memory chip within them. Many of these have a built in USB connection so that transferring the data to a computer is quick and easy.

Alternatively, most computers come with a built in sound recorder. It's very basic, but it does the job: record, save, playback, and so forth. If you're unsure where to find it, try Programs > Accessories > Entertainment or type 'Sound recorder'; into the Search function.

It doesn't offer editing facilities but then, neither did the old tape recorders. For that, you can download free software such as Audacity, which provides a wide range of editing facilities. Think of it as an audio version of a word processor, enabling you to cut, copy, paste and delete sections of sounds just as you would with text. Like a word processor, it will allow you to enhance the product by, for example, amplifying parts or adding more bass.

Most of these facilities are of more relevance to presentation and performance (see Chapter 6) than to exploration and investigation. However, sound recording also allows for the analysis of spoken language. At its simplest level, students can listen again and again to selected texts and comment on the way words are spoken as well as their meaning, a key area of language study as well as a much overlooked one in literature. Ask two or more students to record the same piece, be it prose, poetry or dialogue from a play. Play back the recordings and discuss the differences.

As part of the exploration of poetry, students can decide the best ways to deliver a text, marking a paper copy accordingly and then making their recording. Keep recordings for other classes (and subsequent year groups) to hear. A full description of the case study 'Analysing the language of poetry through *podcasts*' can be found via the link on the Continuum website.

Sound recording and playback can also be used to help students work on spelling and pronunciation. Here is a recording of 'better' and 'gutter'. In the first two recordings, the speaker omits the T sound (be'er and gu'er) and in the last two, the T is clearly sounded. Some students will find this interesting and be encouraged to see *as well as hear* the different sounds they make.

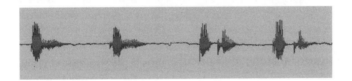

These kinds of facilities also offer many possibilities to the teacher and student of language studies at a higher level. See Chapter 6 for a further exploration of sound recording.

Exploring and investigating together

In an era of social networking, where to have a Facebook account is as common as having a phonebook entry, Web 2.0 technologies are familiar to students and readily accessible. What they offer to English teachers are new and efficient ways of sharing. Collaborative work has long been one of the approaches favoured by teachers but its effective use is often hampered by the logistics of the classroom and, sometimes, by the inability of students to see its relevance. 'Electronic sharing' overcomes these obstacles.

Anna Richardson, a teacher in a comprehensive school in Coventry decided to use the facilities afforded by online sharing in order to help her students investigate literature. To do so she set up a wiki which allowed her to communicate with students in and out of school time and for students to communicate with each other. A wiki is just one of a range of shared online spaces, from Facebook to YouTube to Wikipedia itself – and the school learning platform can also serve this purpose too. This has the additional advantage of being a 'walled garden' accessible only to those the teacher admits.

Initially the teacher used the wiki to set questions and gather responses from students:

> • I began by uploading the poem 'Havisham' on to the wiki and created a page with a number of resources that I would normally have delivered to the class myself. I uploaded a PowerPoint which I had previously delivered to other classes on the poem, a set of questions, some notes in a word document and two links to useful websites which analysed the poem. I briefly showed the students how to use the site, got them signed up with their own usernames and then set them off to answer some fairly difficult questions. They had to use the resources on the site to answer the questions. It was up to them which resources they used from the site; I deliberately did not specify this. I also briefly introduced the students to the discussion pages, encouraged them to communicate with each other this way in order to get some answers to the questions. I also used the discussion tool as a plenary at the end of the lesson: I gave them a question to which they all had to post a response.

She soon realized that the most useful tool was the discussion area.

> It was the response to the requirement to discuss 'Song' (by W H Auden) that confirmed to me that using a wiki was extremely beneficial. Suddenly, lower ability year 8 students were reading a poem for meaning and giving their own personal opinions, explaining their views in detail, using quotations, commenting on language and offering alternative interpretations. Most importantly, students were now interrogating the poem themselves, asking questions and explaining things to each other.

One of the key factors in this was student anonymity. The teacher knew the identity of each user (and could moderate messages if necessary) but they could protect their own identities from each other. This seemed to free students from the fear of being thought either too brainy or too stupid.

The result was a startling growth in independent learning and a confidence in their ability to work things out themselves.

The full report of this project 'Building learning power with wikis' (including a guide to setting up your own wikispace) and a number of others using collaborative technologies can be found via the link on the Continuum site. For more about collaborative work using wikis and other methods, see Chapter 7.

In conclusion

In this chapter we have seen that ICT is a powerful tool in the hands of both student and teacher. A word processor can be employed to do more than type and correct spellings: it can really process words. By hiding and revealing parts of a text or scrambling a text in different ways, we can provoke analysis and discussion. By searching it for specific features, we can help students discover interesting features for themselves. Similarly we can offer students the means of systematically investigating spoken language and visual images. We have also seen how the facility to interact afforded by Web 2.0 applications can be harnessed to engage students in fruitful discussion and collaborative learning.

It should, then, be clear from the many and varied examples in this chapter that ICT offers an enormous range of possibilities for students and teachers to explore and investigate texts of all kinds. Many can be employed straight away using no more than a laptop and a projector. Others will take more practice and the willingness to learn about a new piece of software or a new way of using familiar software. None of the techniques described here or elsewhere in this book (see, e.g. Chapter 5: Using ICT to Transform) is beyond the capabilities of any teacher of English and none require new or expensive equipment. All offer new, effective and engaging ways of exploring and investigating.

2

Using ICT to Analyse Language

Analysis and English teaching – at first sight not the most creative of combinations! Yet you can see statistical approaches everywhere.

You can literally 'see' statistics in Wordle, perhaps the most visually accessible way to view analysis of text by frequency.

And you can spot statistical methods in collapsing, or alphabeticizing a text, now widely used to re-present or deconstruct a text.

Statistics inform the modern dictionary. No longer do lexicographers chew pencils and stare into space to come up with word definitions. Instead they use powerful computers to analyse huge collections of text (a 'corpus') and then read the resultant stats to gauge a word's range of meanings, its collocations and its dominant patterns in the language.

This approach has led to a whole new area of study – Corpus Linguistics. Again, using computers, researchers count frequencies, identify patterns and sort text according to keywords. New discoveries and insights emerge all the time.

There was a time that these methods were the exclusive preserve of academics with access to the sophisticated technology required. However, there are now many free websites that offer you an entry into this brave new world. But for small-scale experiments we can use Word and Excel, and free programs such as AntConc, to achieve modest results of our own.

So, what can statistical analysis offer the serving English teacher? Are there any special advantages for students? Can we use it to enhance the reading of poetry? What about creative writing?

This chapter will explore what Corpus approaches and concordancing software can offer the English classroom – without pursuing the crude numbers involved, or the pseudo-science and jargon associated with corpus linguistics, interesting though it is. By contrast, we are looking for critical insights, creative spin-offs, ways of bringing to the surface inspirational patterns and revelations that have a direct bearing on the classroom.

Wordle

As a place to start, and for immediate dramatic effect, Wordle is hard to beat. It illustrates very succinctly why English teachers ought to consider these approaches. It works by counting the words in a text, assigning a fontsize proportional to the frequency and then displaying the result in an attractive way. It ignores certain words (the 'stop-list') and doesn't include super-common words such as 'the', 'a', 'and' 'to', 'you', 'he' and 'she'.

Wordle is free. To try it out, you simply navigate to www.wordle.net, click on the **Create your own** link and paste in a text.

Here's Keats' 'La Belle Dame Sans Merci':

You can see the Wordle effect with this fairly short text; key words are emphasized and the result gives an impression of the poem.

What happens with longer texts? Wordle displays the top 100 or so lexical words, so a proportion of the text will disappear. You are left with the important words, judged by frequency, from a whole-text perspective.

With longer texts, and especially texts from the past, it is important to be aware of how Wordle works so that you can adjust its output for the most useful results. What follows is a short case study, using Romeo and Juliet (both a long text, *and* one from the past).

This is the result of pasting in the whole text of Romeo and Juliet:

The immediate effect is attractive; you get a brief listing of the main characters, and the most frequent words are proportionally prominent. So Romeo and Juliet are obviously key players . . .

A closer look throws up some anomalies:

- Romeo appears twice, in upper case and lower case
- If you look carefully you can see two Juliets too
- The word Enter is strangely prominent
- The words 'thee', 'thou' and 'thy' are very prominent

Why these effects? A moment's thought gives us the reason. If you paste in a whole play script, some words are *by definition* repeated artificially – the character names in the margin and stage directions. These will distort frequency counts considerably. In the edition I was using, all the margin character names are in upper case – and you can clearly see the effect in the display.

What about 'thee', 'thou' and 'thine'? Wordle ignores common words, but it wasn't programmed to handle ancient texts, so 'thee', 'thou' and 'thine' come out as very important words in Romeo and Juliet.

Actually, an English teacher would like something more revealing. To be honest about it, we don't learn very much from this display of the text.

Here's a fixed version, without stage directions, without margin character names and without 'thee', 'thou' and 'thine':

Much better! The important themes of the play now rise to the surface – the opposition of love and death, night and day. The centre of the play is Romeo.

Wordle is clever – if you don't want a word you can simply right-click on it to remove it and the program will instantly recalculate the display for you.

I'd be tempted to work over this version even more, pruning out little irrelevant words – but for an immediate display, to analyse and talk about, we are almost there.

If you want versions of Shakespeare plays with just the text (margin character names, character lists, scene headings and stage directions deleted) you can pick them up free from Teachit's Word Kitchen (The Word Kitchen is on the Mini site menu – when you get there, look in the Store Cupboard). You will need to adjust words like 'thee' and 'thou' yourself.

Wordle works by frequency counting, and it is quite possible to pick up the stats from the program, copy them into a spreadsheet and work with them yourself offline. To do this click on the 'Language' link.

This gives you a series of useful options. The top two choices affect the way the program deals with upper case and lower case (for the Keats example, I converted the text to lower case). The last option allows you to see the frequency counts, and copy them to a spreadsheet if you wish.

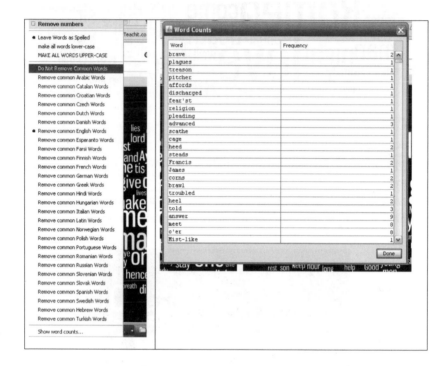

You can also make Wordle count and display *all the words* if you wish to see the prominence of the little words too. To do this choose the option 'Do not remove common words'. Certain texts will be very dramatically revealed if you show pronouns, for instance. You may have to remove determiners and prepositions manually as explained, but it'll be worth the effort.

Here's Browning's 'My Last Duchess' with the pronouns retained. You could note the prominence of the overbearing ego ('I' and 'my'), the focus on the duchess ('she' and 'her') and context of conversation ('you'). Why is 'if' so frequent?

Using a corpus to investigate language

As I said in the introduction to this chapter, a corpus is huge collections of texts analysed by powerful computers. Researchers read the resultant statistics to gauge a word's range of meanings, its collocations and its dominant patterns in the language. Everyone with access to the internet can consult a corpus, since a number of big corpora are freely available for public use.

The process of using a corpus to investigate language is absorbing, fascinating and can become an obsession. What truths and structures exist in all that mass of language that no one has yet discovered? It has the pleasure of a treasure-hunt, the addiction of a crossword and the intellectual satisfaction of real discovery – all rolled into one.

The range of applications in the classroom is also vast, and can cover all areas of English.

In the rest of this chapter I will introduce possible research leads. However, once the class has grasped what the whole thing is about, they will be able to generate their own investigations without too much difficulty.

Some of these ideas simply flag up curious patterns of language use and invite speculation. A corpus may or may not be useful. Other ideas would be enormously extended with corpus use and could lead to mini research projects. The key thing is to engender with your class a habit of mind – a sense of curiosity about language and a thirst to explore and investigate patterns that emerge. A corpus gives you the tools to *apply* this kind of thinking, with immediate source to data to prove/disprove or extend an idea.

Students should as quickly as possible be allowed to own the process – to conduct their own searches and form their own hypotheses. Whether these ideas are technically speaking correct or not is not as important as the process of thinking, speculating and articulating ideas. These habits of thought can also be applied to the study of literature. Because this is a field of genuine research, there are no pre-set right answers, so it's an ideal place to start inculcating the routines of autonomous investigation and hypothesis making.

Try this: Using a corpus to enrich a critical reading of a poem

A wonderful side-product of an online corpus is its ability to enrich our understanding by giving us a quick insight into the associations carried by specific words in a variety of contexts. Applied to the study of literature, it allows us to focus on particular, numinous words and phrases, research them in isolation from the text and then return to the text, intellectually alert to their meaning-potentials and actively thinking about patterns of usage and the associated imagery and suggestions evoked by the writer.

Activity outline

This technique involves the following stages:

- A close reading of the text (preferably in electronic form on screen, or best of all, a combination of onscreen and paper formats)
- Identification of phrases that seem to catch the eye ('Target Phrases'); that appear to conceal information; or in any other way signal interest (this process is as much gut instinct as anything else and needs practice and experiment – some leads turn out to be dead-ends, others reap rich harvests of association and meaning). Mark each one for examination
- Analysis: Students type the target phrases into the online corpus and review the results, asking themselves these sorts of questions:

  - *What contexts are associated with the phrase?*
  - *What other words are friendly with the phrase? – near collocations*
  - *Are there any inseparable friends? A best friend?*
  - *Do you spot any patterns? (write them down!)*
  - *Is there a reason for the pattern? Can you propose a theory? What can be seen in the words?*
  - *Invent a theory to cover what you can see (your hypothesis)*

- Go back to the original text and apply the results to it

- Quantify (if possible) the enrichment of reading and understanding that this process has given. This is best done through whole class discussion.
- Ask students to return to the Hypothesis and test it further using the corpus
- Modify the hypothesis in the light of what is found
- Has that led to further enrichment of the reading?

For all the above, the process is experimental – there may be some wonderful insight waiting; there may be nothing obvious.

However, without testing the ideas using a corpus, it's impossible to know. The key thing is to try it out. Applying these ideas to a study of 'Heaven-Haven' by Gerard Manley Hopkins, we might proceed as follows:

Read the poem and mark the phrases for analysis (see stage 2 above):

Heaven-Haven
A nun takes the veil

I have desired to go
   Where springs not fail,
To fields where flies no sharp and sided hail
   And a few lilies blow.

And I have asked to be
   Where no storms come,
Where the green swell is in the havens dumb
   And out of the swing of the sea.

Note – I found that it was phraseology of a general nature that proved most fruitful. Looking up specific vocabulary in a corpus may not lead anywhere – for instance, predictably, 'sided hail' is unlikely to produce anything at all.

Why did I mark those particular phrases as Target Phrases? I will run briefly through a reading that led me to the Target Phrases – though I am taking you through my thought processes and wouldn't expect students to choose in the same way. Their reasons for marking a phrase might just be a hunch, and although I am sensitive to literature and can argue for my ideas, when it boils down to it, my marking was also a hunch – a corpus is a world of magic so it encourages word-adventures and trips into the unknown!

Here's my reasoning, for fellow-teacher consumption. The nun declares her intentions through a series of statements couched in the negative – building an accumulated sense of self-denial:

springs *not* fail . . . *no* sharp and sided hail . . . *no* storms come . . . the green swell
is in the havens *dumb* . . . *out of* the swing

She seeks a world of reliability, protected from violence, uninfluenced by the powers that sway the rest of the world. The sea is 'dumb' in the haven; its voice silenced. Hopkins calls the ocean the 'green swell', working in the pun on swell to imply the naked life forces of 'green' nature: sex, pregnancy and procreation; all of which the nun wants to be silent, since she is turning her back on their siren song. Can we confirm the range of meanings in 'swell' using the corpus? What would typing in 'swell' or 'the swell' reveal? So that gets my first mark.

So where do we locate the positive? By inverting the negative statements we arrive at some elements – for instance there are no storms, so that must mean peace; she is out of the swing, so that must mean she is in a state of stillness. Apart from that we have a reference to the unfailing spring (perhaps in turn a reference to the woman at the well in John 4; Jesus offered her water so that she would never thirst again) and a strange mention of lilies. It is so odd, it cries out investigation. That gets my second mark.

Another prominent feature of the poem is the parallel opening phrases of the two verses, echoing each other:

> I have desired to go
>> And I have asked to be

This is the language of petition, formal word order. I was struck by the first example. The word 'desire' haunts the poem, hinted at in storm and swell and even lily (overwhelmingly powerful in scent and voluptuous allure, but also a symbol of purity – another example of 'containment'?). In the formula, 'I have desired' the word 'desire' seems exquisitely contained. The language of petition and submission (she has desired, but not demanded, is reconciled to another's decision) controls and neutralizes the subversive potential of 'desire'. Does the tense also contribute? Past perfect. Decided. Done. Resigned to the outcome and the idea?

And again, concealed in the simple language we have hints of profundity – desiring to **go**, asking to **be** – these are two facets of the spiritual haven, one that represents an active escape, reached by a journey of the soul, the other a state of being, where noise and movement cease.

The two opening phrases deserve investigation, so I put them down too.

Lastly, the phrase 'Out of the swing' seemed to echo existing idioms – we talk about being 'out of the swing of things' when we mean we're out of prac-tice – so I wondered whether a corpus would yield any more associations. However, this example throws up an important issue. Usage changes over time. Was the phrase 'out of the swing of things' current when Hopkins was writing, or introduced much later? Most online corpus engines can't tell us that. If date is obviously pertinent to the investigation (any research on the word 'gay' would reveal markedly different associations if the source data is more that 40 years old) it needs to be discussed with the class and the implications considered. These are issues that affect literary study especially.

Are the atmospheric effects observed in this poem borne out by other associations? A corpus may be able to tell us.

So the experiments might follow this order:

1. 'swell'
2. 'A few lilies'
3. 'I have desired'
4. 'I have asked'
5. 'out of the swing'

So that's the routine – identify target phrases and then look them up experimentally in an online corpus.

A free online copy of The British National Corpus is housed at Brigham Young University. You will find it at http://bit.ly/te_17 (or you can call it up easily by typing **bnc byu** into Google). There's a search window and you simply type your phrase into the box and click on Search.

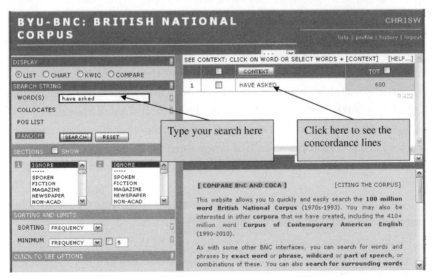

Source: Davies, Mark. (2004–) BYU-BNC: The British National Corpus. Available online at http://corpus.byu.edu/bnc.

A result, in upper case letters will appear in the right hand pane, showing you how many times that term was found. Click on it to see the concordance lines. These will be arranged with the target phrase underlined and in bold.

Source: BYU-BNC: The British National Corpus.

You can copy and paste the results from the search into a word processor to print out classroom resources of your own. Of course, if students have direct access to the system they can read and interpret the results online. However, with a very large corpus there will be material that could be considered unsuitable for some school use. This is because the text-collection will be spread as wide as possible, including adult fiction. With younger pupils it may be wise to adopt a cautious approach and check the searches you ask them to make in advance.

As a case in point, the word 'swell' in my list of searches produces concordance lines that refer mostly to waves of the sea, but it seems to be a favourite word for Mills and Boone, romantic fiction writers, when describing a shapely woman. Not entirely irrelevant, therefore and a well-chosen example of this usage would bring out the sexual/procreative other-meaning suggested by Hopkins. It is clear however, that if one were using these lines with a class-room full of children, one would have to be careful to avoid an unsuitable, erotic line.

As yet, no one has produced a freely available corpus, without overtly adult material, that could be used by schools.

(There are more sophisticated searches: one of the most useful is the use of wildcards. To see words associated with a phrase you can use a 'wildcard' by typing *. Thus, typing 'happy *' would show you all the words that immediately follow the word 'happy' after the computer has searched the

100 million word collection of texts. Typing '* happy' would show you all the words that come before 'happy'. You can use more than one wildcard, for instance 'happy * *').

Using an offline corpus

The online corpus approach means working with a preexisting set of reference texts, and although you can limit the choices to a certain extent, you do not have control over the composition of the corpus.

It is quite possible to obtain concordance software that will allow you to investigate your own text collection *offline*. The very best examples cost money. However, an extremely useful free concordancer is available for download. It is called AntConc (http://bit.ly/te_26). You can install it on you own computer so you don't have to be online to use it. The first task is to assemble the texts you want to investigate. These have to be in text format (.txt). Luckily there are many sources of these texts – Project Gutenberg offers all its vast collection in text format, and it is easy to build a collection of classic texts this way. If you were about to teach the Gothic or Pastoral, or you wanted to find quick cross-references for Shakespeare or Dickens, you could assemble the 'collected works' in a special folder for use with AntConc.

When you launch the program, you first load these texts. Searches are lightning fast, even if you have 30 or 40 novels loaded. Impressive! The output comes in the form of statistically sorted concordance lines, and you can export the results of your search as a text file for import into a word processor.

The program will give you a word list with frequency counts, will let you see collocation patterns, and will even allow you to compare one text with another one to identify 'key words' that have special prominence in each text. AntConc is a powerful tool for creating really exciting new classroom resources, and will repay the effort required to learn its features.

Working with concordance lines in a word processor

If you've retrieved raw concordance lines from a corpus, what you'll have is a series of lines, each containing the target phrase somewhere in the centre of the text. It would be nice to get control over the lines – to display the target word(s) in the centre of the page and have the option of blanking out the target word(s) to make exercises and introductory lesson materials.

How can this be done simply? Well, using standard Replace routines, a lot can be achieved.

Here's a typical sample from a corpus, retrieving the phrase 'have asked to':

United in typically forthright fashion. 'We have asked to be kept informed of Alan Shearer's situation in

the Deputy Prime Minister. The union is believed to have asked to see Mr Prescott this evening.

only national Under-16 competition and 20 counties have asked to be involved in representative football. Younger

full-time staff members who, after a short time, have asked to reduce their hours to entitle them to the credit.

London, has already been moved and seven others have asked to be rehoused after they were identified in the

s report, published last week. Two of the families have asked to be relocated outside the borough, Greenwich council

the men believed to have killed Stephen Lawrence have asked to be rehoused because they fear for their safety. It

---

See what I mean?

This is fine, but unwieldy. It would be best to put this into Table format, each row having three cells and the middle cell containing the Target Phrase. The techniques for making this resource using Word can be found on the Continuum site.

Try this: Use a corpus to investigate word order rules

A corpus can very quickly provide hundreds of examples of word-patterns to enable you to create active lessons where the rules of the game are deduced by pupils rather than given by teachers.

Some of these patterns of use will be familiar – adjectives preceding a noun, for instance. Others will be relatively new to you, and may occasionally be new discoveries known only to you and your class of researchers!

In this activity, students simply investigate colour words:

- What sort of words team up with colour words? (the collocates)
- What order do they go in?

- When there are several adjectives working together, what position do dimension or 'size' words take (big, little, huge, tiny etc.)?
- What are the rules?
- What happens to the meaning if the normal order is changed?

For instance, your students may find instances of this word order:

Little green eyes

(possible rule: colour word usually precedes the modified noun; dimension word comes first in the order)

Then what is the effect of breaking the rule?

Green little eyes

Insult? A sense of the sinister? The word 'little' is doing the job of belittling, of diminishing status. A bit, like saying of someone 'he's a funny little man' when the person in question may in fact be physically big?

Some collocations are dominant. Both Little Green and Little Red have overwhelming associations. Little Green collocates with 'men' – and the alien connection seems to be sprinkled through many of its other contexts. Little Red collocates with – you've guessed it – Riding Hood! But also with book, corvette, rooster and light. Why is there always a 'little red light' on the dashboard? So what would we find with 'little black', 'little blue' and 'little yellow'?

Try using a corpus to give you a list of collocates for a colour word. For instance, for blue. This gives you a harvest of such expressions as 'poison-bottle blue' and 'kingfisher blue' – some juicy metaphorical language to discuss, play with and use as models for creative writing!

Fascinating stuff!

Try this: Odd-Man-Out

This is an activity designed for students who have already had some experience using a corpus.

It requires students to look for and establish the dominant pattern of use of a specified phrase so that they can then identify where the usage is being subverted or played with.

Almost always these examples give an instant display of stylistic skill: they will embody techniques that can be easily copied, learnt and appreciated.

If a writer has deliberately chosen to subvert the current usage of a phrase it is a fair chance that he/she will try other verbal tricks. It's like an indicator of playful style.

As a teacher, these examples can also offer you plenty of other things to talk about – in a context of genuine discovery and 'hooked' interest. You'll find the full range of techniques on display – figurative language, irony, sound effects, strongly patterned word order and so on.

Use this activity to encourage stylistic experimentation (especially for students who are very cautious in their use of language), playfulness, wit, subversion and fun – often the hallmarks of high quality journalism.

Once you have identified the Odd-Man-Out usages as a class, you can print them out, stick them on the wall and display student versions in a cluster round the printout. Allow time for the class to admire other students' efforts – and in so doing assimilate the 'tricks' behind the aberrant usages!

To get a better picture of the task, have a look at worked example:

- State-of-the-art

What are the dominant patterns of use for 'state of the art'?

The concordance lines overwhelmingly show these collocations – computers, technology, kitchens, systems. But there are some clear exceptions!

Examples of Odd-Man-Out, playful usage:

The presumption is that it has to be that big to be so good -that every extra ounce expands what is traditionally referred to as its sheer gaming power. This, however, is not the case. Cantering through the Xbox's capabilities with the **state-of-the-art** alien massacre Halo and the snowboarding dude-a-rama of Amped, I and the men grew slowly deflated.

'I thought I was going to the land of Oz,' Joe said sadly after an hour of Halo. 'This is just Oz from Auf Wiedersehen, Pet.'

Note, the *context* is still computer/high tech.

The French facilities were often a state rather than **state-of-the-art**. During Black's time at Metz, the centrepiece of the training ground was a red ash pitch akin to the ones dotted around schools and housing schemes in Scotland's cities.

Sports facilities often associate with 'state-of-the-art' – here the play on words is between the phrase 'in a state' and 'state-of-the-art'.

> Two big beefcakes make large dents in horror films with oddly similar ghouls. Blade II is a slick and marvellous vampire movie that tears through the sewers and dungeons of Prague. Invincible is a plodding satire that charts the resistible rise of the Nazis. In terms of pure evil, there's little to choose between **state-of-the-art** bloodsuckers and the beer-guzzling Hitlerites of Weimar Berlin. But the hunky heroes of these films are chalk and cheese. In Blade II, Wesley Snipes is as cool and lethal as an icepick. By contrast Jouko Ahola – the 'invincible' Jewish blacksmith who embarrasses Aryans with his feats of strength – is as charismatic as a carthorse.

Why does the reviewer refer to the film vampires as 'state-of-the-art blood-suckers'? Is it implying that these characters are in some sense manufactured, technical creations?

Notice the well-worked word play, the matched compound words (state-of-the-art and beer-guzzling) the alliterative pairs ('hunky heroes', 'chalk and cheese' and 'charismatic as a carthorse'), the similes (ice-pick and carthorse). All of these effects can be copied and experimented with effectively!

> Ross, on the other hand, is perfect for and is running a pretty much exemplary chat show on Friday nights – but is scheduled against So Graham Norton on Channel 4, the only other halfway diverting chat show in Britain. You've just got to put that kind of thing down to a drunken bet rather than the decision of well-paid professionals, because that ain't no way to run a railroad.
>
> No such problems for Theroux, to whom the BBC gives When Louis Met . . . a clear run on Tuesday nights as a mark of their pleasure with him.
>
> Theroux is pretty much **state-of-the-art** chat in 2002 – his trailing-C-list-celebrities-for-a-month schtick succeeding Graham Norton's saying-rude-words-to-B-list-celebrities schtick as the chat methode du jour.
>
> At its best it does make fabulous television. Anyone who didn't come into work the next day squealing about his Jimmy Savile and Paul Daniels documentaries had, frankly, not watched them.

This is quite a distance from the usual haunts of the phrase! Here it is describing a chat-show format. Can you argue that this is also a manufactured thing?

Notice how the journalist has played with another aspect of the target phrase – the hyphens – to make up two long hyphenated compound adjectives. What do you make of the use of the Yiddish 'schtick' and the French 'methode du jour'? What effect is the writer after when he uses words from foreign languages? And what about his use of the surprising word 'squealing'?

> Everything of any significance is now hailed as being **'state of the art'**. Can anyone explain exactly what is meant by the phrase and how it came into being?
>
> **'State of the art'** has two meanings. In advertising it is intended to indicate that a product includes all the most recent improvements; in patent law it signifies all the relevant knowledge before the making of an invention. The European Patent Convention, Article 54, reads:
>
> (1) An invention shall be considered to be new if it does not form part of the state of the art; (2) The state of the art shall be held to comprise everything made available to the public by means of a written or oral description, by use, or in any other way, before the date of filing of the European patent application.
>
> Thus on the strict patent law definition, a 'state of the art' product would include old technology only, not the most recent developments. And Japanese car-makers, who praise a new model by reference to the number of patentable inventions in it, would appear to be offering better than 'state of the art'.
>
> As to the history of the expression, it is a literal translation of the German Stand der Technik, which has been a concept in German patent law at least since 1900, with substantially the meaning now stated in the convention. 'Art' evidently means manufacturing art, like Technik, not aesthetic art. Before 1977, when the convention was set up, the corresponding English and American expression was 'prior art'. It is thus likely that 'state of the art' came into advertisers' usage after 1977. (Kenneth Chapman, Darlington)

By chance, the database throws up a definition! Notice how little the origins of the phrase affect its current uses!

> Barenboim, I discovered, rehearses the Berliners in their mother tongue. My own attempt at **state-of-the-art** Dorset – 'Clarionet, you'm playin' too vaarst! Oi be zubdivoidin into vour' – would no doubt please the traditionalists in the orchestra. I have even featured in a controversial movie.

Here the author uses the phrase ironically – there is nothing in that use of Dorset dialect that suggests modern and up-to-date: the reverse is true!

You could set the class this task:

Can you think of an ironic use of 'state-of-the-art' where you mean clapped out and old-fashioned? For example, you might say 'My Dad has a state-of-the-art computer – it runs Windows 95 but struggles with XP, fine with elastic band, but not a chance of broadband'.

Try this: Turn of phrase

One of the most impressive aspects of a corpus is the way it reveals the complexity and richness of what seem simple combinations of words – the range of meanings, the subtleties and nuances can be astonishing.

This activity sets out to give pupils a creative introduction to corpus use and to show them, enjoyably, the impressive range of meanings in common expressions. They find a phrase with a range of meanings – and then write a creative piece that includes the full range so that the meaning of the phrase mutates – 'turns'.

You could introduce the lesson like this:

- Show a typical search for a phrase you've already tried
- Discuss and group the instances (using a Word table is ideal)
- Isolate the main meanings. Aim to find more than three. Five is ideal.
- Issue a list of possible target phrases
- Ask children to log on and retrieve their own concordance lines
- They too should isolate three or more meanings
- The task is to incorporate the meanings (not the concordance lines!) into a piece of writing of their own, making a deliberate attempt to illustrate the various senses of the phrase in as witty a fashion as possible.

Follow-through

Where the process throws up an interesting grammatical pattern, you can capitalize on it by weaving it into your teaching.

Avoid asking children to look up individual words – always choose phrases. Because of the size of corpus databases, single words will deliver tens of thousands of results – completely overwhelming and counter-productive.

How do you find useful target phrases? Well they seem to occur without too much trouble in every other sentence! For instance, I used the phrase 'throws up' – and it immediately strikes one: 'What's the metaphor behind the phrase? What other meanings are carried by it? Nausea? Discovery? Physical action?'

This phrase provides good raw material for a poem. You could set this task: write a poem that has to incorporate the phrase in every section.

You can read the poem I wrote (not a particularly good one, I hasten to add) as a model, based on five main strands of meaning as defined by a corpus search.

Throw Up

I throw up my hands
In despair
    in shock
    in horror
In ultimate defeat

My life conspires to throw up
Surprises, problems, difficulties
    and
Unexpected shattering conclusions

Living every day throws up
Faults in character,
    Embarrassing blemishes
    Half-healed scars . . .
No good concealing them.
They rise, dark, half-hidden whales,
To the surface of my eyes
From the deeps of long-gone wars
Like ghosts of sunken battleships.

And no matter that I try
To throw up a palisade
The outside world still lobs
A sudden grenade
Into the foxhole
Wrecking everything I've made.

It makes me want
  It makes me want

    to throw up.

Chris Warren

Preposition dance

This investigation explores the way prepositions work with verbs to give us in English a wide spectrum of meanings and nuances, of implications and subtleties. The activity has the added benefit of cementing in students' minds how prepositions work.

The idea is simple.

- Make a long list of prepositions as a class brainstorm.
- Choose a common verb.

- Match it with each preposition.
- Investigate each variant in a corpus.
- Each variant will carry several meanings. Make a list of the meanings and the common collocations for each variant.

For instance, prepositions such as 'in' 'out' 'up' 'down' 'to' 'by' 'off' 'on' 'through' can be matched with common verbs such as 'eat', 'sit' or 'run' to produce a preposition dance:

Eat in	**Sit** in	**Run** in
eat out	sit out	run out
eat up	sit up	run up
eat down	sit down	run down
eat to	sit to	run to
eat by	sit by	run by
eat off	sit off	run off
eat on	sit on	run on
eat through	sit through	run through

Students can ask themselves these sorts of questions:

- What contexts are associated with the phrase?
- What are its collocations?
- Are there any words that _always_ occur with the phrase?
- Do you spot any patterns? (write them down!)
- Is there a reason for the pattern? Can you propose a theory? What can be seen in the words? Invent a theory to cover what you can see (Your Hypothesis)
- Where appropriate, return to the Hypothesis and test it further using the corpus (e.g. try the same preposition with another verb to see if it has the same effect)
- Modify the hypothesis in the light of what is found

Try this: The phrase dictionary project

One of the principal commercial uses of a corpus has been in the construction of dictionaries – based on real contemporary usage rather than a compiler's hunches. An obvious use in class is to set up a project to do just that – make a special dictionary.

Divide the class into say, 10 teams of lexicographers. Allocate each team a set of letters of the alphabet. Give a few starters for each group.

The task, rather than the already-done-to-death compilation of meanings for individual words, is to make a dictionary for _phrases_. It may be best to limit the scope of the investigation to phrasal verbs – still plenty to look at!

⇨

If a whole English department were to allocate a few lessons to this project and a number of classes were involved, an impressive mass of data could be gathered – as it is, one class can a cover remarkably wide area.

The method would be as follows:

- Look up the target phrase in a corpus and list the principal meanings it carries
- List its associations and any patterns that are noticed
- Explore variations that occur when the node word remains the same and the preposition changes – for instance '**run** *in*' '**run** *off*' '**run** *out*'
- Expand the phrase if an idiomatic expression is observed, and check that too (e.g. looking up '**come** *off*' someone notices that 'wheels come off' occurs frequently and looks it up. Sees that 'the wheels come off' can be taken literally, or used metaphorically to mean that plans go awry – especially the progress of teams in football competitions). A good way to do this is to explore a simple two-word phrase, and then very quickly expand it to three or four words when you see the collocations come up on screen. For instance, 'come out' collocates with 'of', 'with', 'to' and 'on' – each of which will limit the search and produce interesting results
- Appoint a team of editors to filter, correct and arrange entries sent in by the teams
- Store the information centrally in sortable form as a wiki on your network or learning platform (a spreadsheet on Google Docs would be ideal, but even tables in a word processor can be pressed into service to sort entries).
- Decide how the database can be searched – for instance, in the case cited a little earlier it would be good to find the explanation of 'the wheels come off' under 'wheels' *and* 'come off'. How can that be achieved efficiently?

Why do this activity? Well, it is not done to create a new dictionary. The *process* rather than the outcome is important. True, the resultant artefact will be fun, and can be added to or consulted, but pupils will learn an immense amount about the diversity of meanings encoded in even the simplest phrase. It makes you realize very quickly how inadequate the single-word dictionaries of past generations are. A start, it's true, but as soon as you investigate combinations of words, the meanings multiply dizzyingly, quite beyond the ability of the conventional book format to record. The future has to lie in electronic sorting and retrieval, and in our ability to analyse the relationships formed *between* words, rather than those words taken in sterile isolation and allocated convenient but inadequate pigeon-hole meanings.

You may consider buying a dictionary that has explicitly been compiled using the corpus method: one such is the pioneering Cobuild Dictionary from

Collins. You will find its description of grammar, and the way that it treats definition of words, extremely interesting. The dictionary was constructed to help learners of English from abroad, but it has much to teach native speakers and all users of the language.

The truth is that corpus linguistics researchers have developed extremely powerful analytical tools for us, and if we are to make any prediction about the future, their influence in education is set to grow exponentially – not just to empower teachers, but also to inspire and motivate learners.

3

Using ICT to Respond, Interpret, Reflect and Evaluate

For English teachers, encouraging and enabling personal response has always been as important as developing their students' creativity. This chapter will explore what ICT can contribute to the ways in which students express reactions to a text, a performance or a situation. This is a large area, covering as it does literary and non-literary texts of all kinds, and there will inevitably be overlap with material in other chapters.

Technology offers opportunities to

- analyse and annotate texts, including multimedia texts and their own work
- explore alternative versions of texts, both by the original author and others
- consider the choices made during composition
- capture ephemeral responses
- devise presentations offering reflections on and responses to texts
- edit their own work easily
- create and access support and revision material and examples of good practice

The malleability of electronic text means that all of these activities can be carried out in a non-destructive way. Although this now seems obvious, it is still instructive to compare a heavily annotated copy of an old set text or examination poetry anthology, for example, that you might find at the back of the stock room, or a scholarly edition of a Shakespeare play in which the notes take up more than half the page, with the multiplicity of ways in which electronic text can be annotated and transformed. Not only can a copy of the original be preserved for reference, students can also embed their own comments in a variety of ways without obscuring the text itself, whether by notes that appear and disappear at the click of the mouse or even multimedia presentations that can run alongside the author's work.

Responding, interpreting, reflecting and evaluating are closely related and are all familiar activities for students and teachers. The NATE document 'The Entitlement to ICT in Secondary English' (on which, as the Introduction explains, much of this book is based) distinguishes students responding to and interpreting texts, both spoken and written, to 'develop and demonstrate their understanding and appreciation' from reflecting and evaluating 'language use . . . to refine their own practice and learn from others' (www.nate.org.uk/page/ict_policy). In practice, these activities often take place at the same time, especially when studying literature. A student may create an imaginative response and then reflect upon the ways their own work relates to the original. An older student who had read Swift's *Modest Proposal*, to cite an actual example from the classroom, a might be inspired to create 'A Modest Proposal for removing the problem of drug addiction in Britain whilst simultaneously alleviating the concern of those against animal testing', accompanied by a critique relating her own work to Swift's original. Traditionally, however, they have been delivered in writing – with the danger that every enjoyable stretch of reading or interesting poem becomes tarnished by the realization that 'we have to write about it'. Less formal methods, such as reading logs or journals, can provide a more personal record; ICT adds a whole range of new opportunities, including capturing discussions and comments as they take place. As one student commented after a session discussing a poem online: 'It doesn't really seem like work.'

Text mapping

Readers have always annotated texts. The British Library shows on its website a thirteenth-century copy of Comestor's *Scholastic History* with notes by the monk Matthew Paris – and no doubt school children scrawled in the margins of their papyrus scrolls in ancient Egypt. The advent of the photocopier made it possible to make more creative use of this often furtive and unofficial activity. A short text could be copied and perhaps enlarged to allow students to comment in a range of ways which might be shared in discussion or by display. The word processor opened up a range of ways this could be taken much further. Not only was the text instantly available online or on the school network so that students could all have their own copies but the tools were much more flexible. The word processor provides highlighters in a large range of colours, so that different aspects of the texts could be picked in out in contrasting shades. In addition, the font could be changed to another face, words could be put in a larger size, made bold or italicized. What's more, effects can be overlaid, so that the same word or phrase could appear with highlighting, in a larger size, different font, in italics and bold – thus illustrating multiple effects. English teacher Tony Clifford coined the term 'text mapping' for this activity; just as a map can represent a variety of features in the physical terrain, the digital text map picks out key features in the passage.

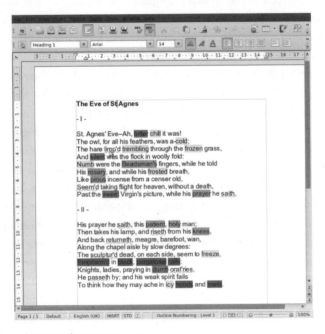

Text mapping using a word processor

As a teacher you may want to model this by using the word processor and a digital projector or a interactive whiteboard (where the tools will offer similar effects) and even start your lesson by identifying the features you would like them to explore. The illustration shows the opening of Keats' poem *The Eve of St Agnes*, with colours used to highlight words about the cold, about religion and also some contrasts (the monochrome screenshot hides the use of five colours in the original). Students are likely to learn much more, however, if they are given the freedom to explore and annotate the passage in their own way. Ask them to annot-ate aspects that interest, intrigue or perhaps puzzle them – and, most importantly, to produce a key to the system they use. If students work in small groups, it will be very instructive to compare the results – ideally, asking them to explain their version of the text while it is displayed to the rest of the class. In one lesson, students should see for themselves that readers respond to texts in many ways.

This technique can be taken further by using the word processor's tools to add comments, footnotes and illustrations. As with handwritten notes in the margin, there is the danger of over-annotation; students can be shown the virtue of concentrating on a limited number of features, if necessary producing more than one map or version of the text. These activities should feel like straightforward extensions and enhancements of familiar paper-based activities. Special skills and software aren't needed and texts can be copied from the internet or quickly typed in. The technology has, however, more to offer still.

Try this

For more suggestions on ways to dig into a text with a word processor, see the online activities for Macbeth's speech 'He's Here in Double Trust' on the area on the Continuum site for this book (http://education.rank.continuumbooks.com). These include using tables and how to use the speech to create a found poem.

Enriching the study of texts

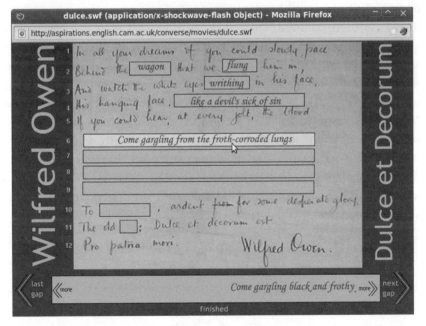

Exploring Owen's drafts on the Converse site
Source: Converse from Cambridge University: aspirations.english.cam.ac.uk

The internet does more than make available a vast library of texts. The riches of some of the world's great libraries such as the British Library are also coming online to enrich the study of language and literature. Precious manuscripts, discarded drafts, mementoes and ephemera that have been too valuable, fragile or simply too far away can now be accessed by students to explore the ways in which authors create their texts. Just as teachers have learnt the dangers of setting the task of 'finding out something' about a topic, leading to information overload (or possibly paralysis for students confronted with an avalanche of search results), these resources need mediation if students are to make fruitful use of them. Oxford University's First World War Poetry Digital Archive (http://bit.ly/te_11) has over 7,000 items of text, images, audio and video on this much-studied period. For higher education students the 'Introduction to Manuscript Study' provides a wealth of material and an activity on the ways an editor creates a version for print. For most, although the resources on this site are fascinating and provide rich material for guided study by older students, the choices are too daunting. Cambridge University's Converse site (http://bit.ly/te_12) demonstrates how the same materials can be used to create a highly effective guided activity. Students work with a version of Wilfred Owen's 'Dulce et Decorum Est'. They are asked to look at the choices that Owen made in drafting and redrafting the poem, and consider what difference the choices made. They do this by working on an image of one of Owen's own handwritten drafts from which key phrases and lines have been removed. Once they have dragged onto the spaces their choices from the various alternatives that Owen himself considered, they are presented with the final version of the poem and a tool that allows them to add their own comments on the differences. As the introduction to the activity says: 'This resource isn't about trying to get the poem "right"', but rather to focus on the process of composition. In the process it illustrates vividly that a poem rarely springs forth whole from the writer's brain (or pen) – and if writers often go through many drafts, the least readers can do is take these choices seriously. There is also a lesson about the value of redrafting their own work, of course, which we shall come to later.

Poets in their own words

The Poetry Archive site is a rich resource for teaching poetry.

Source: The Poetry Archive: poetryarchive.org

English is about more than words on a page, of course. Everyone can learn a great deal just by reading aloud – and as the Australian poet Les Murray says, 'A true poem is dreamed and danced as well as thought.' This comment appears on Les Murray's page on the Poetry Archive (www.poetryarchive.org), which describes itself as 'the world's premier collection of recording of poets reading their work'. The site offers much more than that, but just hearing the poet's own voice can transform appreciation of a poem, whether it's Murray's Australian twang, the scratchy voice of Tennyson reading from 'The Charge of the Light Brigade' or W. B. Yeats' incantatory reading of 'The Lake Isle of Innisfree'. The poem comes alive, its rhythms revealed, the stresses helping to make sense of the words on the page. Having listened to Murray reading 'The Tin Wash Dish', perhaps following the projected text, students may be inspired to create their own recordings of this poem or others on a related theme. The hardware and software to do this, as Chapter 1 shows, is now cheap and readily available. The Poetry Archive offers considerable enrichment; teachers may like to follow the detailed lesson outline for this poem provided by Sue Dymoke in the extensive section 'For Teachers', which suggests (among other approaches) creating a multimedia presentation with images and sound to match the text. Students may want to explore Murray's other work on the site or the work by another poet suggested in the 'Where next?' section that follows this poem. Locating a poet or poem is straightforward, using the search facilities on the site. Students or teachers who just wish to enjoy listening to poems can create online anthologies in their own area of the Archive; others may want to explore poetic forms or research a poet's life and works. American poets are represented too, thanks to a link with The Poetry Foundation in the USA (www.poetryfoundation.org), a site that provides its own archive and resources. The American site doesn't confine itself to poets in their own voices, stretches back to Chaucer and provides selected readings of poetry across the ages. This brief outline will, we hope, be enough to persuade you to pay a visit to both sites; they are constantly adding new poems and resources.

Try this

Easy access to audio can be invaluable when studying poetry but other texts can benefit too. Martin Luther King's legendary 'I have a dream' speech of 28 August 1963 is rich resource which can be used for a wide range of student activities, including aspects of oratory such as repetition and imagery. A good place to start is the Open University's *Moving Words* website, which has audio extracts and a transcript as well as detailed suggestions and resources. This site contains other useful lesson resources and suggestions for departmental training on using ICT in English: http://bit.ly/te_8.

Exploring the sub-text

The flexibility of electronic text provides opportunities for students to explore sub-text too. When considering motivation, for example, students are often invited to suggest what they imagine the characters might be thinking. A word processor makes this easier to display and complete. Consider the short scene in *Macbeth* where the King invites Banquo to dinner in the evening. At this stage of the play, each character is likely to be wary of voicing their true feelings. A simple way to do this would be to put the text into a table, with space on either side for what is going through their minds – Macbeth sinisterly on the left, Banquo righteously on the right, perhaps. You can do this by using the *table* menu – *convert text to table*, then insert columns on either side. This will produce a cell for each line; if you would prefer more space to comment on each speech, simply select the rows beside it and find the 'merge cells' button. With the addition of column headings, this text can be made available to students who have already enjoyed a reading or performance to work in groups of about three, adding their versions of the characters' thoughts. Presentation software such as PowerPoint enables them to take this a step further, in a technique we've dubbed 'PowerPoint Counterpoint'. With the spoken text displayed on screen, each character can be given their own thought bubbles. These are sometimes labelled 'callouts' in the software; select contrasting colours for the thought bubbles for each character. Then, as students read their parts, the text unfolds on the screen accompanied by these unvoiced reflections and possibly sound effects and images too. The technical skills required are minimal and students enjoy trying out the facilities offered by PowerPoint and its equivalents – though it is still good practice to explore for yourself how to do this in advance of the lesson. The real skills are central to English: the writing and designing of the slides; the writing and adjustment of the performance scripts and practising the finished work to get timing and effects just right. Students should be encouraged to reflect on their work and adjust the text and effects accordingly. You can find illustrations of this activity, including documents to download on the play and Blake's 'A Poison Tree', on the NATE site in a section to support professional development courses from Vital: www.nate.org.uk/page/vital.

A cartoon approach to alternative interpretations

Using online resources to create a Shakespeare storyboard

Source: Bitstrips: bitstrips.com

Teaching different interpretations of a text is difficult. Students often want to be told a 'right' answer; it's perhaps not surprising that some find it difficult to explore different interpretations when they struggle to discover even one. Gregory Anderson, a teacher working in a school in Scarborough, found that storyboarding is an effective way to support the teaching of this important English skill. 'Although skills associated with traditional storyboarding can be developed', he comments, 'there is surely more potential in the use of higher-level thinking skills – that is, of exploring different interpretations. While traditional storyboarding encourages pupils to ensure a clear link between each comic pane, apt punctuation and spelling and some adherence to the conventions of comic strips, the potential of ICT allows interactivity and collaboration.' He used the free online tools at Bitstrips (www.bitstrips. com), where it's possible to save and revisit your work. This makes it easy to create a simple representation of a scene such as Romeo overhearing Juliet at the balcony, complete with their words in speech bubbles:

Juliet: O Romeo, Romeo, wherefore art thou Romeo?
Deny thy father and refuse thy name,

> Or if thou wilt not, be but sworn my love,
> And I'll no longer be a Capulet.
> *Romeo*: Shall I hear more, or shall I speak at this?

Students are shown how to choose different expressions or body postures and reflect how these might indicate different ways of feeling about the event. Individuals or groups can rapidly create their own interpretations and then display and discuss them side by side in class. As Gregory remarks: 'This is perhaps the most important teaching point: to emphasize that although the *words* are not changed, their *meaning* does depend on expression or body language.' Students enjoy the interactivity and see its value as well; one commented: 'It helps you visualize what you put down . . . it helps you remember what you thought about, and it helps you relate the characters to pictures . . . which helps me remember the story.' As it's possible to save the storyboards, email them and have them printed out, students can have a record of their work for display or even revision. Gregory explains in detail how he set up and extended this activity in his case study, 'Interpreting texts through interactive storyboarding' which you can find in the area on the NATE site on 'Making hard topics easier to teach with ICT' (www.nate.org.uk/htt). There are other storyboarding and comic creation sites on the internet, some of which offer secure accounts for education. As with all such online activities, you'll need to check the site in advance and keep an eye on the students' computer screens – though the best policy is to ensure that students have clear guidance on their task and learn how to operate safely online. This should be a matter of whole school policy on safe use of the internet (or 'e-safety'); if you (or your students) are not clear about this, make it your business to find out.

Getting the picture

Images can provide another kind of response as well as stimulus. These can be pictures selected by the teacher to provide context for a literary text, or perhaps to generate discussion and illustrate alternative interpretations. Images have a multitude of other uses in the teaching of English, such as creative stimulus or as the subject of investigation when studying, say, advertising or media representations. The ability to display full colour high quality images in front of the whole class is an obvious way in which digital technology is a real advantage, though that is only part of the story. It is perhaps worth noting at this point that the easy access to a vast array of images through a quick search is a challenge as well as an opportunity (something else that should be the matter of whole school policies). Whether the image is to be used for whole-class display or by students on their own, it is usually wise to either have a small collection of pictures already available or to provide carefully selected links. Many web images are also of low quality – poor copies or too small for enlarged display. It is however possible to locate some fabulous treasures, such as the William Blake Archive (www. blakearchive.org). Your school or college may already have a subscription to an educational image collection such as the ones provided in the UK through regional broadband consortia or JISC (www.jcs.nen.gov.uk); these are worth exploring, as not only will the images be of good quality and copyright cleared for use in education but they are likely to be easy to search and come with background information; even a date can be very useful information. Illustrations of literary texts can provide rewarding material. Paintings of scenes from Tennyson's popular poem 'The Lady of Shalott' by artists such as Waterhouse and Holman Hunt are a case in point. Displayed on a whiteboard, they furnish not only visual representation of many details of the text but also the opportunityfor plenty of exploration. The interactive whiteboard will allow you or your students to annotation aspects, ask questions and provide links. Why, for example, do some paintings show the lady entangled in her embroidery? What do students think the images tell them about the situation of the woman? Which lines from the text would they link to an image? Students can have their own copies of the images to annotate, using either their own copies of the whiteboard software (it is usually possible to install this on student machines so that their work can later be displayed to the class) or by using simple 'callout' tools provided in a word processor.

Try this

If you'd like your students to explore 'The Lady of Shalott' in detail, you'll find a number of valuable resources on Ed Friedlander's site (http://bit.ly/te_10), including several paintings and copies of the versions of the poem Tennyson made in 1832 and 1842, which could provide further material for study.

Software allows images to be annotated in a variety of ways

Source: Photograph by Tom Rank

The photograph of the elephant demonstrates other ways images can be used in the classroom. This might be the focus of work on detailed description ('skin wrinkled and grey like . . .') or a short piece of creative writing ('the elephant is thinking . . .'). Alternatively, students could record their views on keeping animals in captivity – and in all these cases, notes can be made on the image itself. One of the assets of whiteboard software is that it not only allows easy annotation but also provides a means to save these for future use – in a later lesson or for homework, for example. If you are using an interactive whiteboard, you should also be able store further relevant pictures in the whiteboard gallery. Any picture can be quickly dragged onto the page, or a new page, to provide further stimulus – perhaps showing campaign images from animal welfare groups alongside promotional material from a zoo. One of the features of interactive whiteboard software is that it permits annotation and screen capture of anything on display so that it is possible to use the tools on web pages, leaflets in *PDF* format and more. This is a valuable way of exploring many aspects of the media, from news sites to advertisements. Some versions also allow capture from moving images, so that it is possible to freeze and annotate a film of a Shakespeare play, for instance, providing another tool for exploring texts.

Moving on

This approach can be taken further, allowing students to recreate digital content for their own purposes. One of the benefits of developments in software and hardware is the way it has reduced the barrier to the creation of media in schools. This means that as well as watching a film, students can not only capture images by using freeze-frame software but also cut up sections of a film and create alternative versions. The film ceases to be a 'lean back' medium, in Marshall McLuhan's phrase, as students select key extracts which they can then manipulate in various ways, including changing the background soundtrack, adding narration, slowing down or speeding up the film, even altering the order of events. Although this requires some training in the use of video editing software (basic versions of which are now available at low cost) and the time required means you are unlikely to do this often in mainstream English lessons, it should give students an understanding of how film and video are produced and an awareness of the differences between printed and moving image version of the same story. We are now aware that 'literacy' covers more than simply an understanding of the written word; in the age of mobile phone videos and YouTube, students need the ability to evaluate and criticize what they see and hear all around them. Making their own short movies, whether using existing material or filming their own, gives invaluable insight into the processes as well as the product.

At a school in Birmingham, for example, Angus Weir wanted to help his teenage students understand and respond to Stevenson's classic story, *The Strange Case of Dr Jekyll and Mr Hyde*, which many found challenging because of the language, structure and setting. Adopting a problem-solving approach, he set the students to create trailers for a fictitious computer game based on

Jekyll and Hyde and a detailed justification and reflection document. Their preparation included both close reading of the text and watching three video game trailers: *Resident Evil*, *Silent Hill 2* and *Haunting Ground*. They then mind-mapped the conventions of these games so that before starting to create their videos they had a clear understanding of the characters and plot events of *Jekyll and Hyde,* the genre conventions of Gothic and Gothic-influenced computer games and a clear idea of their task. Having created their trailers, watched them and evaluated their own work and that of other groups, students gained in confidence as well as understanding. One commented: 'Choosing to have our trailer narrated meant that we had to concentrate on snippets of text and assess how dramatic they were. When you see our final video you can see that we've had to think about the effect the words have on the audience.' In an interesting insight into how ICT enables new ways of assessing and recording work, even in an informal way, another wrote: 'As I can put the video file on my phone it allows my parents to see it and this also helps me get confidence.' You can read Angus's case study on 'Teaching the literary heritage' on the NATE site (www.nate.org.uk/htt).

Online reading journals

The comments by these Midlands schoolchildren indicate how responding often culminates in reflection and evaluation. As teachers, we often want students to capture their initial reactions, perhaps to reflect their changing experience as they progress through a novel, or their first thoughts on an issue so that they can reflect later on how their ideas have developed. Reading logs and journals are often used for these purposes; the advent of shared areas and learning platforms can make it much easier to monitor and share these records (and simpler for students, too, to keep track of their work). Rebecca Darch, working on a class reader with 12-year-old students in a London school, found that the forums in her school's learning platform provided her with a valuable enhancement of the traditional reading journals. The method she adopted was to create a 'thread' for each student, which meant that it was possible to follow their individual entries while making the forum accessible to others so that they could, if they wished, read and respond to comments by other readers. She found that it provided a means to engage those students who do not readily volunteer: 'In the feed-back at the end of the project many girls commented that sharing work "improved confidence". An interesting development occurred at this point, the students began to add a comment to me, stating whether or not their journal entries could be shared with the class. I found that they enjoyed the sense of empowerment that they achieved from choosing their own activities, and whether this could be included in my lesson.' Rebecca also noticed that because students soon felt at ease in this informal environment, their work would be a fairer reflection of their real interest; some able students were soon doing far more than the stipulated task, creating additional activities. One commented: 'You could express your thoughts and feelings on the book in many different ways.' A more hesitant reader's brief summaries alerted the teacher to the kind activity she felt more com-fortable with, enabling the teacher to ensure that there was more support and encouragement in future sessions. Another very successful activity was an online development of hot seating: she selected some of the more confident students to respond to question in role as characters from the novel. The discussions continued well after the scheduled end point because students were so engaged. It also encouraged students to develop independent work – often a real problem when dealing with a normal size class. Once Rebecca encouraged students to come up with their own questions about the text, she found that questions she had previously considered too difficult were raised spontaneously and discussed freely. You can read her complete case study on the NATE site: www.nate.org.uk/page/lp.

You will need to find out what facilities your institution has for this kind of work; learning platforms (or virtual learning environments – VLEs) offer this in different ways, or you may be able to create secure blogs or wikis. A wiki is, essentially, a web page that can be edited by users. There will be a more detailed exploration of wikis and how to use them in class in Chapter 7.

The popularity of podcasts

More public forums can also encourage students to invest considerable effort. It is often hard to predict what will really engage recalcitrant stu-dents, but teachers have found that the ability ICT offers for students to publish their work for a real audience, whether inside our outside the school, can inspire reluctant contributors. Sometimes the motivation is personal, such a blog about a hobby or sports team, on other occasions external assessment may be the spur. When Carrie McMillan wanted to help her classes explore the language of poetry in closer detail for external examinations, she decided to make them the experts. She capitalized on her students' skill and enthusiasm for group exploratory talk by asking them to create podcasts about poetry – digital audio files, made available on the internet for download by computer or personal mobile devices. The hardware and software to enable this is now cheap, free or even already supplied with the computer, so that it is possible to create recordings with only basic equipment (though of course if your school or college has facilities such as a studio you can achieve better results). In the process of planning and creating a podcast, students will use a range of strategies, from formal writing for planning, scripts and note-taking to plenty of unscripted discussion. The final podcast may be scripted, improvized or a mix of both. Carrie discovered interesting contrasts between her two groups. Those facing a public examination in a few weeks were strongly motivated by the discussion aspect and by the end-product of a revision podcast and less interested in the editing process. The question and answer format had particular value in forcing them to address the details of the text to justify their answers – a crucial skill that less able students often find hard to master. Those in the year below, by contrast, were highly enthused by the prospect of tailoring their work towards a teenage audience, incorporating stylistic devices they had picked up from their own radio listening and in the process revealing an understanding of how the media target their audience. In each case, of course, students can evaluate their own productions, comment on work by other students – and benefit from the work of students in other years, too. Here too you will find the details on the NATE site, including detailed help sheets on using the free audio software Audacity that has already been mentioned in Chapter 1 (www.nate.org.uk/htt). There is also a very helpful introduction called 'Assignment: Podcast' on the BT Education site which is based on using Audacity. You and your students should find it very useful – some, of course, is in the form of a podcast (http://bit.ly/te_6). We should make it clear that while this kind of activity takes time and hard work, students often find it great fun. Those who are really fired up can be encouraged to develop their skills further.

Try this

Perhaps your school could have a regular news podcast on the website? With a cheap hand-held recorder (such as an iPod with a clip-on microphone) students can interview each other, school staff or older members of the community, or capture 'vox pops' from around the school on – well, just about anything, from how many students have breakfast before school to whether they think the voting age should be changed. Editing is carried out on the computer, where students can add voice-overs, sound effects and music which they can either create for themselves or download from a number of sites offering free resources. We provide links to some of these on the accompanying website.

Editing for beginners

Audio and video recording enables us to capture the kind of ephemera that can so easily be lost in discussion and role play as well as enabling the production of items to publish in a variety of ways. ICT has also made it much easier to record fleeting events in a variety of other ways. Class improvization and role play can be captured with a digital camera and quickly transferred to a computer for reviewing or reporting group reflections on a character or situation. Students' written work can also be recorded. Simply by using the ability of the word processor to 'track' or 'record' changes, the teacher and the writer can see the extent and nature of the editing and revision process, although this level of detail can be overwhelming and few students will want to engage in this kind of reflection. An effective use for this facility is far simpler: allowing students to review and record their suggestions on each other's work. Students are naturally anxious if they think that someone else in the class is going to alter – nay, ruin – their writing. The ability to record multiple versions can overcome this fear. One approach would be to use this with a lesson in which students all have access to a computer and where you know that students will feel comfortable allowing others to respond to their work. Establish some ground rules: the first draft of this writing will be read by someone else in the class (you may wish to determine the pairings rather than leave this to friendship groups) and any suggestions or alteration must first include at least one comment on what the reader has enjoyed about their partner's work. After they have completed an initial version, they save this in their own secure area and move to another computer. They turn on 'track changes' (you should find this in the Tools or Edit menu) and then amend their colleague's writing, using the 'add notes' facility to leave comments where appropriate. If desired, this edited version can also be saved with a new name. Everyone returns to their own work, where they consider the suggested changes, each of which the original writer can decide to accept, modify or reject. Clearly there are many opportunities for the teacher to observe and become involved in the results of this instant feedback, far quicker and in many ways more relevant than 'marking' returned days later.

A more public way to engage in the challenging process of editing and redrafting is by using the visualizer. One student described this as 'a camera on a stick'. Even a basic version, operating directly to a projector, allows the instant sharing of students' own written work. This makes it possible to share the kinds of discussions about the task we often find ourselves repeating several times to individuals during a lesson, with an example visible for everyone. Quick edits by student or teacher can be demonstrated as they happen; as the visualizer shows this, the class can then add their own comments. Phil Grosset, who makes extensive use of the visualizer in his classroom, describes its particular advantages as 'spontaneity, interactivity, variety and its contribution to classroom management'. As well as displaying text, for example, it can provide graphic displays of objects such as chocolate bars and drinks cans when studying branding and packaging, You can see a short video of Phil using the visualizer with his class in the Teachers TV film 'Hard To Teach – Secondary English Using ICT' and his case study on the NATE site. (www. nate.org.uk/htt).

Taken on trust?

Reflection and evaluation are skills that students need to learn when reading published works as well as their own writing. Now that the internet is the first source of information for so many users, it has become even more important to encourage discrimination when assessing the reliability of what students read and view. If they have become familiar with the ways in which online resources are created – for example by creating their own wiki pages – they will be able to discuss how far it is possible to trust the reliability and authenticity of entries on sites like Wikipedia. Beyond that, of course, there are many sites which promote points of view about politics and issues such as climate change and animal rights. This may be a fruitful area to work with colleagues in other subjects, since the ability to detect bias and test the accuracy of information is important across the curriculum. The internet, while presenting challenges, also provides an easy way to compare materials. In the past, you might have only had access to one or two sets of encyclopaedias in the school library and a few other reference texts.

Try this

Ask students, in groups, to compare what they can find on a topic – for example a writer – in the reference books in school with online resources. To make the activity manageable, you'd need to assign them one or two sources each and provide them with a set of questions they could answer quickly and present in a meaningful way, such as:

- How long did it take to find the right information?
- How many words are there on the topic? (Tip: copy and paste the text into a word processor for a quick word count.)
- When was it written?
- Who published it? (This could lead to an interesting discussion of 'publishing' on the internet if you wish and have time.)
- What illustrations does it have?

You might want to dig a bit deeper by also asking students how accessible they feel the articles are, if they contain information on a particular aspect of your subject (such as an incident in an author's life: 'What costume with headdress was Byron painted in, and why?') and inquiring about value judgements. One long article on Byron, for example, remarks: 'His quarrel with orthodoxy neither alarms nor provokes the modern reader.' 'Modern', here however means 1911, as that edition of the *Encyclopædia Britannica* is now freely available on the internet; it should be instructive to compare it with the latest edition, also available online with an institutional subscription (selected entries, including the one on Byron at the time of writing, are also available to everyone). If you can include a few other sources such as *The Oxford Dictionary of National Biography*, depending on the access in your institutional and the abilities of your students, you should have material for rich comparisons on matters such as the relative merits of anonymous or named writers, up-to-date information and so on. Don't forget to stress the importance of correctly citing reference works; *Britannica* and the *ODNB* both provide ready-made citations at the end of each entry (students could be asked why each of these details, including the date, is necessary). Students will need to find this information for themselves on many other sites. They may conclude that paid-for information isn't necessarily superior or the best place for all research – but they should have a better understanding of the need to evaluate information from any source. A similar activity could be carried out on sites dealing with controversial topics or comparing news sources across the world for reports of a topical event.

None of this deals with the phenomenon of copying, plagiarism and 'research' that goes straight from web page to essay page without troubling the learner's brain. You will find some imaginative ways to tackle this – not in itself a new problem – in Chapter 5, 'Using ICT to transform'. We hope that the activities suggested in this chapter also offer you a variety of stimulating ways to respond to texts and reflect on topics and in the process avoid students expecting someone will simply tell them what to think and write.

4

Using ICT to Compose and Create

Chapter Outline

This chapter takes composition and creation as its theme and focuses on the power of ICT in enabling creativity and innovation. There are other instances in this book of texts and other cultural artefacts being created or composed. The dialogue in a play script might be composed using the text of a novel or short story; a piece of persuasive writing might be created from a descriptive text – and ICT would be extremely useful in these and many other examples.

However, here we wish to highlight the way in which ICT can be harnessed to encourage or enable **new** material, **innovative** texts and **imaginative** creations – rather than re-creations.

Sometimes ICT is perceived by teachers of English as antipathetic to creativity and imagination, perhaps because of its genesis in binary code and the world of technology and mathematics. (Though mathematicians, understandably, would be among the first to claim creativity for their own!) This chapter will show that far from being the enemy of creativity and flights of fancy, ICT can bring all sorts of new opportunities into play and can be especially useful in helping students who see themselves as less able or less imaginative to re-evaluate themselves.

The chapter will consider ways in which ICT can help

- in generating ideas
- organizing and reorganizing those ideas
- in experimenting with composition
- to broaden horizons by opening up the possibilities of non-linear composition
- to offer creative options through the use of mixed media/multimedia

Generating ideas

'Me 'ead's empty, Miss. How do you get ideas?'

How *do* you get ideas? Some people are lucky: ideas just seem to swim into their consciousness in shoals. Others stare around at a vast empty ocean. What we do know, as teachers, is that the generation of ideas and alternatives is aided by variety of stimuli and the opportunity to play.

Sounds and images

At the most basic level, teachers have found that using a projector to display interesting, arresting or sometimes simply random images is a helpful starting point.

One of the simplest ways to do this is to display pictures from a selected folder on the computer connected to the projector. From Control Panel select Screensaver and choose My Pictures Slideshow from the drop down menu. You can browse to a specific folder into which you've placed appropriate images. You can also choose how long to display each image and how long the computer needs to be idle before the display begins.

Most sound file players will display abstract pictures while music or other sounds are played. Such images might not be useful when trying to help the generation of ideas but may come in handy at other times.

Some use music in the same way. Type 'random music' into a search engine and see what comes up. For example, Wolfram Tones is fun and can be adjusted for the style of music you want, though, like many of these sites or programs, the output can be repetitive after a while. Another alternative is to use

PhotoStory 3. Import a few images of any kind – they can indeed be random as they don't need to be seen: they are only there to allow you to access the screen where you can 'Create Music'. This produces 'music' in many styles from Urban Funk to Classical and in all sorts of moods. Of course, you could simply gather a sufficiently large collection of suitable tunes on your computer or MP3 player and select 'shuffle'.

Ideas from words

Random words

For most teachers of English, ideas are generated by words. Is there any point in displaying random words? Possibly, depending on the context of your lesson or if you just wish to encourage play, which as we know is one of the ways in which we experiment, explore – and learn.

Watch Out 4 Snakes.com provides a collection of 'Creativity Tools' which will be of interest to the word-lover and the lover of the surreal (http://watchout4snakes.com). Random Word Plus allows the user to select from noun, adjective, adverb, verb (transitive or intransitive), interjection or preposition. It also allows a choice from 'Very Common' through to 'Obscure'. If you choose obscure interjections, be prepared for 'Willikers!' while common nouns will provide a more familiar fare.

Of the other options, I have found the Random Sentence Generator the most likely to evoke responses, whether 'How can a fume save the oriental owner?' or a host of others. Random Paragraph Generator could also be of interest: with these kinds of resources you always need to try them and see what use they might have.

For a simpler generator, try RandomWord.com, which generates nouns only (http://bit.ly/te_13). My first six were: subway serviette plankton spoon ark dressmaker. I could envisage these as the starting point for a story or a newspaper report, perhaps asking students to select at least three from a given list. Remember to write them down as they are generated (or have students remember them – one each) as there is no way of going back to review an earlier word. The site's section on 'How to use the random word technique for brainstorming' is worth reading.

The Random Word Generator at fourteenminutes.com interprets 'random' in a different way, creating new words for you (http://bit.ly/te_14). You have the option of suggesting the initial letter or letters. For example, if you are looking for random words beginning with 'bl' you might get:

blact	blisel	blunctried
bloomy	blans	blamanther
blams	bloccultings	blacher
blacknitchles	blumsive	blassabite
blesthamentionalless	blenly	
blably	bluringly	

Possibilities for Jabberwocky-related creations immediately spring to mind, as do activities where students are invited to come up with definitions for these words. And don't let me find anyone being blumsive about it.

Words in context

Many teachers will be familiar with 'word clouds' where a group of words is displayed, generated from a specific context such as a poem. Wordle is perhaps the best known of these and can be found at www.wordle.net. The instructions are simple and the results attractive:

There are a few variations which mainly affect the appearance of the word cloud. It is possible, however, to fine tune the process so that common words are omitted, as in the given example.

It is also possible to retain phrases, as in this example from *Jane Eyre* where the 'red room' is described.

This is done by inserting a tilde (~) in place of the spaces between words. To save time, select a phrase, and hold down Control while selecting the other phrases which you wish to keep intact. Then go to Find/Replace; find a single space and replace with the tilde. Your text should look something like this:

> If I profane with my~unworthiest~hand
> This~holy~shrine, the~gentle~sin~is this:
> My lips,~two~blushing~pilgrims, ready stand
> To smooth~that~rough~touch~with~a~tender~kiss.
> Good pilgrim, you~do~wrong~your~hand~too~much,
> Which mannerly~devotion~shows in this;
> For saints~have~hands~that pilgrims'~hands~do~touch,
> And palm~to~palm~is~holy~palmers'~kiss. (etc.)

One of the options is to show all words as lower case, which we have selected here so that 'sin' for instance appears only once, rather than once with a capital and once without. The resultant 'sin' is, in consequence, also larger. (You can artificially increase the size of a word by inserting a colon followed by a number after a word. Try it.)

To harness this simple function in a more interactive way, ask students to decide which words to link together. They will enjoy trying out the various possibilities and when they are satisfied, their results can be saved by using 'Print Screen' and pasting the image into a word processor, PowerPoint or Paint. Different students' or groups' interpretations can then be shared and discussed. Decisions as to colour, font and alignment can also be questioned.

Those interpretations deemed the best can be printed, enlarged and posted on the wall. A quick and easy way to create a classroom display!

Given that Wordle can be set up to remove common words or leave them in, students could also be permitted (or perhaps encouraged) to delete words which they see as unimportant, while keeping a record of their deletions.

An underused function of Wordle is its word frequency counter. However, this is not the place for such investigations, which belong more properly in Chapter 3, 'Using ICT to Analyse Language'.

Another application of a similar type is Word Fractal. This application is currently available on the Teacher Resource Exchange http://tre.ngfl.gov.uk/. Type 'fractal' into the search box and a link to Word Fractals will appear. Click that to see the description and scroll down to download the Word Fractal zip file. The author describes the use of the application with primary children but there are as many or more uses at secondary level.

Word Fractal will take no account of word frequency and is quite likely to produce a massive 'their' and a tiny 'Tyger' so you might want to edit the words entered quite carefully, removing 'the', 'their', 'of' and so on. Alternatively, click Try Again a few times – or delete any words you don't want. The pictorial background can also be varied by clicking on it.

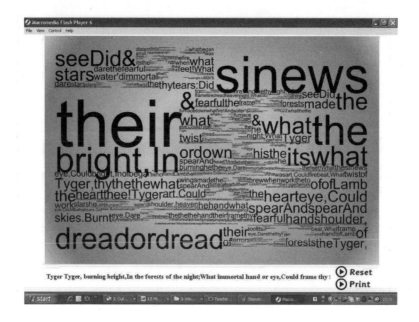

The application will also randomly join words together: 'dreadordread', 'handsshoulder' or 'hearteye', for example. You can see this either as a disadvantage or another way to stimulate the brain.

There are applications which claim to generate poems – rather like a fruit machine. They tend to produce lines such as these:

> ALL FLOWERS BUY FAST, DARK STREETS.
> SKYSCRAPERS STOP LIKE DARK RAINS.
> NEVER FIGHT A DOOR.
> THE FAST DOOR QUICKLY HUSTLES THE JOB.

While this can be amusing for a while and could be useful as a means of spotting the odd line which works or which inspires other ideas, the best use of such generators is to inform a discussion about writing and especially poetry. Are these texts poems or not? Why is 'skyscrapers stop like dark rains' an unsuccessful comparison?

The most satisfying poem generator I have discovered is the Dylan Thomas Random Poem Generator on the BBC Wales website (http://bbc.in/te_15) which seems to throw up lines which are more interesting than 'never fight a door'.

For example:

> And mildly the blush of the horses
> Kiss impatiently in praise of the fisherman

Trotting while they cover
Heartily into the lazy farmhands

This can lead into a discussion about phrases which they feel are '**good**', '*OK*' or 'RUBBISH'.

And mildly **the blush of the horses**
Kiss impatiently in **praise of the fisherman**
Trotting WHILE THEY COVER
HEARTILY into the *lazy farmhands*

Students can then create a text for themselves and make what alterations they feel would improve it and result in a poem. Would it really be a poem? Who had written it and why? What is the difference between something which sounds or looks quite good and something they have written themselves completely? Or something a poet has written?

Try this

Generate a random poem as above and ask students to use it as a starting point for their own poem. They might indicate by use of bold or italic, those words which were part of the original, or, if they are mainly pruning and rearranging, ask them to comment on what changes they have made.
  A 'generated' poem might look like this:

The trotting bones of the night
The viperish street in flesh,
Missing by the star-struck sunhoneyed bottle
For blazed leaves blaze
With no more eyes than the saucebottle

But be turned into something better, like this:

The trotting bones of the night
In the viperish flesh-street,
Miss the star-struck sun-honeyed day.

Organizing ideas

In adapting random lines of poetry, we have begun to move on from idea generation to the organization of ideas. This is a fruitful area too – though there is a lot to be said for spidergrams and similar proven aids on paper or flipchart, or whatever comes to hand. Many teachers make use of the interactive whiteboard software which allows them to capture quickly written spidergrams, lists or random bullet points: a useful facility and a saving on flipchart paper.

What can ICT offer in the area of organizing/structuring ideas?

- Interactive whiteboard software to capture handwritten suggestions
- Word processors to rearrange items into different groups/alter priorities
- PowerPoint slides which can be rearranged like index cards
- Programs which are designed to facilitate 'visual thinking' and the organization of ideas

At some point in the writing process, an order has to be established – unless the creator is attempting a non-linear hypertext approach, of which more later. In speaking, this is even more the case; try creating a non-linear spoken report (or listening to a non-linear speaker).

Word processors

A word processor is a highly flexible tool for the management of ideas once they are turned into words. While they do not allow words to float anywhere on the screen, word processors do offer a simple way to organize a range of items into an order. They also provide straightforward ways of signifying importance or subsidiarity.

Here's a list of ideas about 'Cars – good or bad?' It could be the starting point for a talk or a report. It might result in a debate, an essay, a PowerPoint display – who knows? Whatever the outcome, the items need to be organized.

Cars are cheaper when you are transporting a family
Cars use up dwindling resources
Cars produce fumes which are dangerous to health and pollute the atmosphere
    and add to global warming
Cars encourage a selfish attitude
Cars are necessary in rural areas
Cars enable people to visit their friends and relatives
It's safer for children to travel in cars than walk or bike
Cars create traffic jams
Cars cause road accidents with loss of life and use of medical resources

You don't get enough exercise if you drive everywhere
You can't do without a car in modern Britain
Car manufacture provides valuable employment

The first stage is to separate the pros from the cons. We might use a high-lighter (red and green would be appropriate) or any other text format tool. Having done that, we could drag and drop the items so that they form two distinct banks. A useful shortcut is Shift + Alt and the up/down cursor (arrow) keys. Just position the mouse caret in the line you wish to move and use that combination of keys.

Cars use up dwindling resources
Cars produce fumes which are dangerous to health and pollute the atmosphere
    and add to global warming
Cars cause road accidents with loss of life and use of medical resources
Cars create traffic jams
Cars encourage a selfish attitude
You don't get enough exercise if you drive everywhere

Car manufacture provides valuable employment
It's safer for children to travel in cars than walk or bike
Cars are necessary in rural areas
Cars enable people to visit their friends and relatives
Cars are cheaper when you are transporting a family
You can't do without a car in modern Britain

Once the items have been separated, they can be prioritized. Some might be sub-sections of other ideas, in which case, use a tab to indent or try using 'Outline View', which offers different levels of importance. It also allows items with sub-sections (i.e. those marked with a plus) to be collapsed:

+ Cars are ecologically bad
    – use up dwindling resources
    – produce fumes which are dangerous to health
    – pollute the atmosphere and add to global warming
+ Cars cause road accidents
    – with loss of life
    – use expensive medical resources

This kind activity is crucial for students to be able to develop into competent writers and needs modelling again and again in as many different ways as possible.

Tables provide another way of organizing material that is flexible and readily available. Create a table like this and drag and drop the arguments for and against into the appropriate columns:

Cars: Points in favour	Cars: Points against
Car manufacture provides valuable employment	Cars use up dwindling resources
You can't do without a car in modern Britain	Cars encourage a selfish attitude
. . . . and so on	

A development of this involves creating three columns. Paste all of the points into the centre column and then ask students to drag and drop them into the appropriate for or against categories:

Cars: Points in favour		Cars: Points against
	Cars use up dwindling resources	
	You can't do without a car in modern Britain	
	Cars encourage a selfish attitude	

Alternatively, the centre column can be used for points which are neutral, such as facts about car ownership or the number of road traffic accidents. You may find it helpful to change the page orientation to landscape.

Similar approaches to the ones described here can be adopted using interactive whiteboard software which will allow text to be moved to any part of the screen, making it easier for ideas to be grouped, tried out and rearranged.

PowerPoint

PowerPoint is seen (and often criticized) as merely a way of making lecture notes visible and encouraging irritating special effects. It is true that it can be used badly – both by students and by those who should know better. However, that should not prevent us from appreciating some of its very useful functions. One of these is the way in which in can help us to crystallize our thoughts and then to arrange them. Slides should only ever contain a summary of what is to be said.

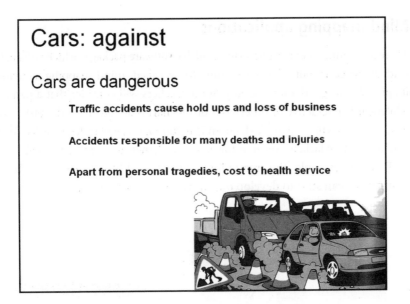

Once ideas, thoughts, points for and against have been jotted down onto slides, the slide sorter view can be used to decide the order in which they should be arranged. This is the case whether there is to be a spoken or a written outcome: the slide sorter is equally useful for both situations and is a facility with which students may not be familiar.

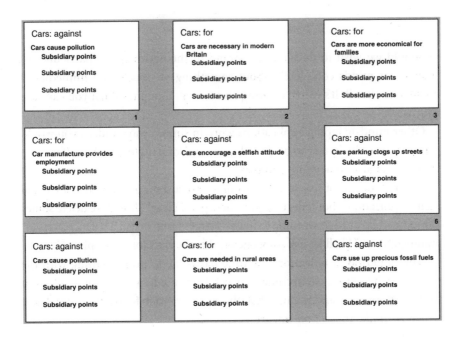

Mind-mapping applications

There are a number of commercially available software packages which will enable students to carry out what have come to be called 'mind-mapping' activities. It's probably as good a term as any. Some teachers will consider that a pen and whiteboard (interactive or otherwise) or flipchart is adequate for the task – and in some cases where a simple diagram is required, this will indeed suffice. What pen and surface lack, however, is the ability to change: to rearrange at will.

Take, for example, the free online application, Bubbl.us (www.bubbl.us). Using it, we can start to develop our ideas for a report on cars.

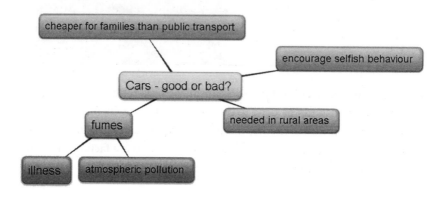

Should we wish to develop one strand of the argument in particular, or change our minds completely about something, it's easily and immediately possible to alter it. It's worth creating an account, though, so that you can save your work.

Other mind-mapping applications work in similar ways and, as you would expect, those which have to be downloaded and/or paid for, tend to offer more facilities but also to be more complex.

The bottom line, of course, is to encourage not just the generation of ideas and their organization – but reflection. Are these good ideas? Should we delete some? Do some really need re-wording to make clearer? Have we got a balanced report/argument/essay? Shall we ask someone outside the class for their opinion?

After a period of reflection, the time has come to do something with the material, whether it is to become a speech from notes, a script for a talk, film or *podcast*, an essay and so on. What, though, if we wish to produce something which is, unlike these, non-linear?

Non-linear composition

A non-linear text can be read in more than one order, usually at the reader's discretion. It is possible, but difficult, to construct these using traditional means. The 'Choose Your Own Adventure' books which were popular in the 1980s and still have a readership are probably the best example of non-linear texts in printed form. The computer has, of course, given us the facility to construct such texts if not with ease, then at least more easily than before.

Without realizing it, we are all familiar with hyperlinks. Anyone who has used a website has clicked on a link to go to another page. Most of us have experienced sites where we have become quite lost, partly because once there are multiple ways of reaching and leaving a page and the site becomes almost literally, a maze. (Not quite literally, of course, because one can always click the back button or a home icon or simply crash out!)

One of the paradoxes of non-linear composition is that it requires careful (usually paper-based) planning if students are to avoid becoming extremely confused quite quickly. I recommend a familiarization activity using Word or a similar word processor before beginning a larger project.

Create a story based on a familiar tale such as 'Jack and the Beanstalk'. Just concentrate on a small part of the story. The plan might look like this:

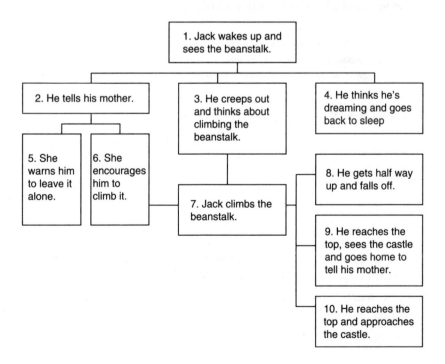

Notice how complex it has already become, especially as there can be more than one route to a particular point in the story. Some routes have to be closed off (e.g. going back to sleep) or the possibilities swiftly become too many to handle! For ease of reference, number the pages.

By the way, the plan was made using text boxes in Word. It could equally well be made on a whiteboard with a pen, as long as you also have an eraser, or using a mind-mapping application.

Planning a story with choices or a non-linear piece of non-fiction is a demanding task which some of your students will enjoy and other will find frustrating; so be prepared to give them assistance.

Once a plan has been made, some text needs to be written before hyperlinks can be created. It is a common mistake to forget that two pieces of text (or two documents etc.) have to be created before a link can be made between them. If students think of building bridges between islands, the reason for this should be clear. In the example given, it would be best to create four documents before we insert hyperlinks. Hence a 'page' describing Jack waking and seeing the beanstalk – two or three sentences would be enough – followed by the three choices.

Create another document and write a little more about action 2. Now do the same for actions 3 and 4. Save all of them. Now you can go back to document 1 and add hyperlinks to each of 2, 3 and 4.

> 1. The next morning Jack woke up early. He yawned and stretched and looked out of the window. What was that? He took a closer look. It was a beanstalk – and it was huge. It seemed to reach all the way up into the sky!

What does Jack do next?

- He goes to tell his mother.
- He creeps out of the house and wonders about climbing the beanstalk.
- 'I'm dreaming', he thinks, turns over and goes back to sleep.

Now link each of the bullets to the choices. Select a bullet point and press Control and K. This enables you to browse to where you have saved documents 2, 3 and 4. Select the appropriate document and click OK. The text will then appear as a link and Ctrl and mouse click will move you to that new document. When you have written documents 5 and 6 you will need to go back and edit number 2 to add choices and links to that, of course. And so on!

You can carry out a similar exercise using PowerPoint, with the advantage that you only need to create new slides rather than new documents.

Don't be put off. Some students will write avidly in this situation when they have chewed their pens in others. As with any activity, consider where creating a non-linear text would be most fruitful. Perhaps it would be in creating an information text: websites provide obvious models, but a branching text would be equally appropriate in Word or PowerPoint. A class studying, say, poetry of World War I could create a PowerPoint within which users could choose which path or line of interest to follow. For example, see the figure below.

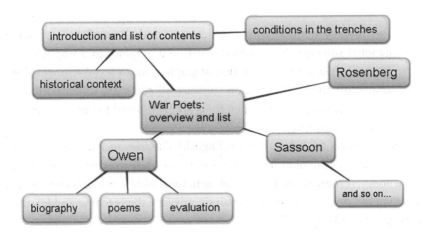

This plan is straightforward in that there are no multiple links. It might, for example, be useful to insert a link from a particular poem back to 'Conditions in the trenches' or from a poem by Sassoon to one by Owen: that, after all, is the point of having a hyperlinked text. Anything of value created in this way becomes a resource for the future, of course.

Mixing your media

Much has been made in the world of ICT of the term *multimodality*, often to impress others. It means a combination of modes of communication, for example, combining graphics, text and audio output with speech, text and touch input. Modern telephony is the application which most clearly exemplifies all these modes. You can touch your phone screen or input text; it will interpret spoken instructions as well as, incidentally, allowing you to speak to one or more people who have a similar device. Its output can also be sound, text or graphics – or a combination of any of these. Were there a way to include taste and smell, these would no doubt be included too.

The concept is not new. We have been combining words and pictures for as long as we can remember. What is new? Three important aspects:

- the ability to include sound and moving images
- the ease with which all of these things can be accomplished, even by very young users
- the ease with which the components *and* their relationships to each other can be changed

We are already familiar with the ways in which PowerPoint and other presentational software can combine words and graphics in a way which is more dynamic than the mere insertion of graphics into a text document. Film strip, animation and video-creation software all add extra dimensions; as a result, the multimodal options open to us are (compared to only a decade or so ago) truly astonishing.

But, we always ask, what's in it for English? The relevance to Media Studies is obvious and the possibilities exciting but are we likely to expend time, energy and money/resources in pursuit of activities which are interesting and engaging but do not, in the final analysis, advance the teaching and learning of English? Read on.

Multimodal possibilities

Film is the most obvious example which comes to mind when considering 'multimodality' as it can embrace sound and moving image, together with text and music. (However, do not overlook the possibilities offered by still images plus sound and music (e.g. PhotoStory) or radio/podcasting which can include words and music, though some purists might question its inclusion here.)

Video (and related media) can be employed to create, for example:

- A group interpretation of a poem
- A presentation of an episode from a novel
- A scene from a play

All of these might be taken from published texts – but consider also making a film of a student's poem, story or play script. The attention which will inevitably be given to language in the course of this work is one of the most worthwhile aspects of this kind of activity: not just a by-product but the most crucial outcome.

Film can also be used to capture moments of drama for subsequent analysis and development; to record talks, group discussion or debates; to record the often overlooked experience of oral storytelling or storymaking.

Moving words and moving images

A class of 14–15-year-old students, studying poetry, used Windows Movie Maker to interpret poems from the Other Cultures section of an exam anthology. Rather than work on a whole poem, the teacher wanted them to focus on language in a more concentrated way and suggested that they select a few key lines and use images to bring out the meaning. Neither students nor teacher were experts in using the software but everyone learnt as they went along, in itself a valuable experience in sharing a learning process.

The application was not hard to use for students familiar with other Windows software; they could also refer to a guide created by CLEO, the regional broadband consortium Cumbria and Lancashire Education Online (http://bit.ly/te_16). The students were encouraged to use real objects to photograph or to film, as well as images from the internet. This was easier for the student working on lines from 'Love after Love' by Derek Walcott than the one interpreting 'Night of the Scorpion' by Nissim Ezekiel. Appropriate music was added together with the text from the poems resulting in short films of approximately a minute and a half which were enjoyed by the other members of the class and could be shown to other students in the year group, no doubt resulting in a chorus of 'Why can't we do that?'

The teacher encouraged constructive criticism, especially where directed at the appropriateness of the interpretations, and students were asked, 'What would you have done differently? And why?'

Students of all abilities tend to engage with projects of this kind, though some may need more guidance, perhaps involving the gathering of images or objects by the teacher beforehand, from which they are able to choose.

The Reporter Reports

A secondary comprehensive school was looking for a way to raise standards in literacy, to engage and motivate boys and to educate students and staff in the use of 'new media'. They employed a film-maker with experience of working in educational environments who worked with students aged 12–13 to create short (2–4 minute) films on topics of their own (moderated) choice. Students were guided in how to research and then how to turn material into workable scripts. Students entered into the project with enthusiasm as they began to understand the need for careful preparation before recording took place. The rehearsal and recording process improved everyone's speaking and listening skills as well as those of team-work and concentration. The recordings were edited by the film-maker, with assistance from students and teachers where feasible, and resulted in entertaining and professional videos.

Pros and cons

The advantages: student engagement was high. Even those who were initially shy of appearing in front of a camera eventually wanted to participate. Literacy skills improved in the areas of focused research, writing to inform (especially non-chronological report writing) and confidence and clarity in speaking.

Staff and students also learnt a good deal about using film as a medium which will inform future work in both English and Media Studies.

Possible pitfalls: the school needs to be equipped with a camera and the software and hardware suitable to edit the film. Also, to enable the skills to be embedded, some staff and students (an expert group?) need to learn how to record and, more importantly, to edit film footage. Most crucially, employing a film-maker for several days can be expensive. Other factors to be aware of: include careful planning and timetabling in order to enable the project to have enough time and suitable rooms/equipment.

Having said that, it is worth looking out for local film makers who may be willing to work with a school at an affordable rate. Many will already be cleared to work in schools ('CRB-checked' in the UK jargon). On the other hand, you may already have expertise in school or within the pool of governors and parents.

Most schools already have the equipment they need and, if not, it is not unduly expensive and should be part of any twenty-first-century school's repertoire. Similarly, software such as Movie Maker is not hard to master and will serve the needs of most English teachers.

Schools which have used film as a tool for teaching and learning English (as distinct from learning about film making or media) report very positive experiences. Perhaps every English teacher has the desire to be a Spielberg as well as having an unfinished novel in the desk drawer.

Animation

Animation is a form of film-making which seems to engage students of all ages. If you have a digital camera and the right software, you can make an animated film. There are a number of pupil-friendly programs available and for the purposes of the English classroom, those designed for Primary use will be more than adequate.

Most examples created by students use Lego or plasticine figures against cardboard backdrops or something similar. It is much harder to create cartoon drawings, though some students will need to try this approach before they will acknowledge its difficulty!

A simple technique which can be utilized to animate words, perhaps to demonstrate an idea to assist spelling or to help with syntax involves Scrabble letters, or any similar tiles from word games. These can be quickly assembled into one order, picture taken, a letter added or moved, picture taken and so on. The activity not only produces 30 second teaching resources but instils the spelling (or whatever teaching point in question) in the minds of the film-makers.

© Trevor Millum

How multi is this modality?

In these examples and others which we can envisage, the finished product is almost entirely one-way. In other words, we have not fully exploited the possibilities of multimodality because the viewer, reader or user is rarely able to interact with it except by turning it on or off, adjusting the volume and so on. The choices available through hyperlinks are the obvious exception.

However, there is, arguably, more to be gained in terms of teaching and learning through students constructing or composing their own artefacts than there is to be gained by responding to those which have already been created by others.

* * *

By the time you read this, other opportunities will already be presenting themselves: new applications, cheaper computers and cameras and access to advice, examples and assistance via learning platforms and wider broadband collaborations, the last of which will also offer wide audiences for the creative materials produced by your students.

Using ICT to Transform

With a word processor, at its most basic, you can do three things:

- Create an entirely new text from scratch
- Edit an existing text to improve its quality or accuracy
- Perform a more radical edit by loading an existing text and setting about transforming it, making changes to its form, content, audience or purpose.

A radical transformation of text puts the word processor through its paces, but more importantly it exercises the brains of the editors to the maximum. A-Level English Language exams have for many years featured such activities using hard copy, coloured pens, sheaves of paper, glue-pots and scissors. Now transformation exercises are featured at GCSE too.

But doing it the 'hard way' with paper and pen means a lot of the mental energy gets diverted to the practicalities of snipping and sticking. A well-designed equivalent activity using a word processor avoids all the fuss of material manipulation while retaining all the intellectual challenge.

Early in the days of ICT and English this transformative function was identified as one of the most powerful ideas on offer because it has so much built into it, and despite the advances of technology in every sphere it is still a key part of ICT and English, especially in the light of the recent specification changes.

In the act of transforming a text you get to know its hidden secrets; you begin to understand its structure, its blueprint; you look closely at the brush strokes that create the illusion! For example, changing the intended audience of a text forces you to acknowledge what that audience is – and what changes will be required to suit the new audience. Both come brilliantly into focus.

What makes the word processor special is that it takes the labour out of the activity. The bulk of the work is done. If you have reasonable skills with the program you can apply all your energy to thinking about the fundamentals of the task in hand, rather than the mechanical effort of typing out the original.

There are other benefits too; if students get into the habit-of-mind implied by the task, if they understand the fundamental malleability of text enabled by a computer, that approach spills over into all editing of text. With handwritten drafts, when the ink dries that's it – the text becomes frozen. The problem is that except for the most dedicated writers, the mind sometimes freezes too – the mental process of working on a text can end as the ink dries. However, regularly practising transformation exercises counteracts this unhelpful habit of mind by illustrating dynamically how changes can be made – and crucially, how exciting those changes can be!

Some might say that text transformation is a species of plagiarism. If we ask students to transform text, are we in fact encouraging the very thing that we ban so vigorously elsewhere? I would argue, on the contrary, that transformation offers us one of the best antidotes to a culture of plagiarism. If we deny the power of technology to make available and to manipulate text we'll be like King Canute, unable to resist the inevitable. The best way forward is to face the facts – look at these world-changing aspects of computers and, instead of banning them, exploit the power for our own purposes. I would like to suggest that if we approach the issue imaginatively we can even use these facilities to counteract cheating and make it far less attractive.

Maybe we shouldn't be saying: 'never borrow text'.. We should be saying: 'if you borrow it, use it, and transform it, *always* acknowledge that you have done so (extra marks available for the acknowledgements)'.

A teacher-set transformation task acts to counter the well-founded fear that ready-made texts can be borrowed by students electronically, given minimal treatment and then submitted, unacknowledged, as original work.

- The borrowing is explicit – all students begin with a 'borrowed' text so no one can start pretending that they wrote it.

- The actual engagement with the text is also quite clear – in order to fulfil the task, students must understand the text thoroughly, and that understanding (or lack of it) becomes immediately evident to an informed reader.
- Mindless transference of great chunks of copied text is instantly made impossible – the task obliges pupils to read, *think about* and treat the whole text.

If we ask students to amass material from the internet on the subject of smoking, we can expect a deluge of undigested, unread copying. If we then apply a transformation to the same task – for instance, that the material must be adapted for a specialized audience (e.g. to make a leaflet for 9-year-old girls) – students will be obliged to read, think about, select from, and modify the material, a quite different affair from simply submitting beautifully printed sheets of unread facts. So if plagiarism is a problem, consider giving each task involving research from the internet, a transformational tweak that makes straight copying impossible.

To summarize, transformation as a process aims:

- To encourage students to develop a high level of skill in editing – with all the reading, comprehension and sophisticated understanding of language that goes with it
- To use the editing power of the word processor, rather than simply using the machine as a typewriter/transcription device
- To establish positive attitudes of mind towards text manipulation and redrafting, so that text is seen as fluid
- To prepare students for a world where text is ubiquitously available, transformable, and applied in thousands of ways every hour of every day
- To give students the necessary mental skills to cope with such a world and to master it for their own purposes rather than just suffering its effects passively

The availability of texts

Internet sites and CD-ROMs offer a wide variety of 'ready-made' texts. Indeed the very availability of so much literature in electronic form forces us to consider imaginative ways of using the resource. Just having the whole works of Shakespeare at the touch of a few buttons is the start of the problem, not its solution!

Practical routine

- Download a text, or a section of a text, from the internet or from a CD-ROM.
- Load the text into a word processor – on a network of computers, you may wish to make the same text available to all the connected machines

- Ask students to analyse and modify the text – *transform* it in the ways suggested here. In so doing they will encounter a range of editing strategies.

What transformations are there? Here's a short, far from comprehensive list:

- Change audience (different age group)
- Change audience (similar age group)
- Change audience (different genders)
- Change purpose
- Change tense
- Change specified classes of words (verbs/nouns/adjectives etc.)
- Change viewpoint
- Change by shortening
- Change by expanding
- Change form
- Change genre
- Change style
- Change historical style – to a past style or imagined future style

The next few pages illustrate the kinds of transformation you can develop as a school resource. They all pre-suppose pupil-access to equipment. Ideally the task should be tackled in pairs or threes, so that the activity generates maximum opportunities for discussion. However, some tasks tend towards individual work and in that case it may be best to book out the ICT suite for a morning.

Change audience (different age group)

Suggestions for activities based on this transformation:

- Technical instructions aimed at adults, rewritten for children
- Safety advice adapted for teenagers
- Children's fairy stories rewritten with an adult audience, and adult sensibilities in mind
- Ancient myths, rewritten (and even illustrated) for young children (Ancient World Web; Internet Classics Archive; Perseus Project)
- An advert designed for young adults adapted for a range of other ages (different groups in the class could work on specific ages)
- Medical advice or advice for young people adapted from adult advice sheets on how to cope with ill relatives (cancer, MS, AIDS, Parkinson's, dementia, etc.)

Changing audience is a classic transformation. You can transform up the age scale or down it. Both present special difficulties and require discussion, thought, and a thorough focus on the audience in mind.

Content

In some examples, you will need to transform content as well as diction and style. For instance, it may be quite acceptable to assume that adults understand the dangers of handling boiling water; so one could omit all references to it if you were writing tea-making instructions for adults. You'd write simply: 'Pour on boiling water'. However, if those same instructions were being adapted for 8-year-olds, an assumption like that would be wrong!

Reading level and 'treatment'

The needs and reading level of the audience must be understood. Writing for a young audience, for instance, suggests simple diction and short sentences. Font size and type must also be considered: the word processor allows not only control of the typological aspects of writing, it can manage layout and illustration too, where appropriate. How far can the form and style of the writing be preserved while adjusting for reading level? Writing for a young audience is especially difficult – not the easy task it might appear. This is a useful fact to establish with a class.

Lesson ideas

Begin by establishing the editing parameters special to this kind of trans-formation. This is best done through brainstorming, through asking questions of the class, encouraging discussion. Record ideas as bullet points.

Thinking about age-level editing may be difficult without some concrete examples to refer to. Try to collect as many examples as you can – look in hospital waiting rooms for pamphlets written for children, then see if you can find the equivalent adult version. Search the internet – which of course has the added benefit that the text comes ready to work on – no tedious typing to do. In fact the exercise depends on having an original ready to transform! We are not talking about creating documents; the idea is to change an existing one.

Texts that could be used for this transformation

Technical instructions aimed at adults, rewritten for children

Tea 1

'How to make tea' can be found on the English Tea Store's website: http://bit.ly/te_18

- What would you do to the text to make it suitable for an audience of 10-year-olds?
- What would you omit?
- Would you change the order of points?
- What would you add?

Tea 2

The article 'Software for tea-making duties', also found through a web search, illustrates how prose written for adults (in this case of American origin) displays distinctive features of its own – shared specialist vocabulary, humour and obsessions with adult issues. This one comes from Wired News (http://bit. ly/te_19). How would you transform this article so that it would be suitable for a British, teenage audience?

Children's fairy stories rewritten with an older audience in mind
Fairy story 1

This version of 'Little Red Riding Hood' can be found on the website DLTK's Crafts for Kids (http://bit.ly/te_20). When you read it, you realize it has already undergone a transformation or two! What details have been changed? Why?

Can you transform this text so that it is aimed at teenagers? What messages might you want to include? Why would you want to transform it? Look at Roald Dahl's *Revolting Rhymes*. What has he done to these stories? Also see Angela Carter's *The Bloody Chamber* for some examples written for adults.

Fairy story 2

A translation of the original Grimm brothers' story can be found on the 'German Fairytale Road' site (http://bit.ly/te_21) or the Virginia Commonwealth University site (http://bit.ly/te_22). How does it differ from the American version?

Fairy story 3

Now compare the first two versions with Perrault's version on the *Classics Illustrated* site (http://bit.ly/te_23). Look at the ending: the moral reminds us that child-abuse is not a new phenomenon, and stranger-danger campaigns had their historical equivalents!

Change audience (similar age group)

Suggestions for activities based on this transformation:

- Article in the *Guardian* – rewritten for the *Sun*
- Article in the *Sun* – rewritten for the *Guardian*

To accomplish this task a student will need to begin appreciating the subtleties of style that differentiate one publication from another, the rules each one works to. No mean feat! Working on a word processor forces an editor to focus on the essential elements in the task, reinforcing understanding and demanding in-depth study of the article in question.

Content
Content will undoubtedly differ, though both articles may be based on the same set of original facts. We'd expect much more detail of the fussy factual type in the *Guardian*. The *Sun* perhaps will cut straight to the story. Thus, the first example will be easier to accomplish than the second – where will students find the extra facts? Perhaps a solution would be to provide a bullet list of details that can act as a 'quarry' for both articles, and then students can decide what material to include or omit.

Reading level and 'treatment'
The needs and reading level of the audience must be understood. Famously, so the legend goes, the *Sun* assumes a reading age of 10, but this does not mean its editorial style is childish; far from it. Diction and sentence length are restricted, but each article is highly crafted for wit and achieves an impact that *Sun* readers have come to expect. It is thus very difficult to write for. The *Guardian* doesn't aim to entertain as much as inform and discuss. You can see that these issues about treatment are both complex and crucial to an understanding of the papers' purposes.

Another key element is the composition of the headline.

Setting up the activity
- Go online: www.thesun.co.uk and www.guardian.co.uk
- Find a news item that features in both online papers. It should exhibit some of the contrasts in style and approach discussed above and ideally be reasonably compact. Copy and paste both articles to separate word-processor pages.
- Get the word processor to count the number of words used in each headline (you may be able to do this by eye!) and the number of words in the main text of each article. You can select the text of the Headline and then select the Tools menu and then Word Count for this (there is a keyboard shortcut for this in Word: hold down both the Control and Shift keys and press G).
- Write these numbers down at the foot of each article.
- Create a third document containing the summarized facts in a bulleted list.
- Set up the task by presenting the *Guardian* text, with its word counts, and asking students to edit the text into a form suitable for the *Sun* (supply the *Sun's* word counts but not the text).
- Students attempt the task using a word processor, without accessing the internet!
- Finally they are able to look at the *Sun's* version and compare their efforts with it.

- End the lesson, if you can, by displaying these files on an interactive whiteboard, discussing any points that occur to you or the class when the various articles are compared – the professional versions and the students' work.
- What was omitted in terms of facts? What was included? How did the writers appeal to the emotions of the reader? Were there any political points scored? How did the papers make use of pictures?

You may find that the online version has already been 'treated' – simplified, shortened, summarized – to suit the format and fit a screen. If you prefer to do so, you can always buy the *Sun* and the *Guardian*, choose your news items, find the internet versions, copy them into Word and then adapt your onscreen text to match the hard copy versions.

If you wish to run the activity the other way, use the *Sun* version and issue the list of facts. Ask students to write up the item in a form that is suitable for the *Guardian*.

Change historical style

Some suggestions for activities based on this transformation:

- Past styles brought up to date: for example Shakespeare modernized
- Present writing transformed into a past style: for example, contemporary prose rewritten in Dickensian style (see Leon Garfield's *Smith*, and William Golding's *Rites of Passage* trilogy for examples of modern writers emulating past styles)
- Imagined future styles: for example contemporary prose rewritten in the style of AD 2220 (cf. *1984* (Newspeak), *Riddley Walker, Clockwork Orange*?)

This process can be practised by 'translating' suitable examples into the target style.

However, some students may prefer the freedom to compose freshly generated material, without reference to existing text – especially if the task is to write in a future style. I would recommend both, since the structure of a piece of text-for-translation provides everyone with a good starting point! When translating into past or future styles, the rule is to choose translation pieces that are short, clearly and progressively structured and where the features of language that the translators will need to emulate are very clearly on view.

Past styles brought up to date: For example Shakespeare modernized
Texts that could be used for this transformation
Modernizing Shakespeare can be a way into understanding both the shifts in culture that make Shakespeare seem sometimes alien to the modern sensibility and the issues that, remarkably, unite us across the centuries making him feel like a contemporary.

If the Shakespeare passage you've chosen is highly structured and with a strong progressive line, the process can be delightful and arouse strong feelings of achievement. Although it may be a little clichéd to us, students encountering the Seven Ages of Man for the first time find an instantly accessible progression. It makes it almost the perfect passage to start with.

> All the world's a stage,
> And all the men and women merely players:
> They have their exits and their entrances;
> And one man in his time plays many parts,
> His acts being seven ages. At first the infant,
> Mewling and puking in the nurse's arms.
> And then the whining school-boy, with his satchel
> And shining morning face, creeping like snail
> Unwillingly to school. And then the lover,
> Sighing like furnace, with a woeful ballad
> Made to his mistress' eyebrow. Then a soldier,
> Full of strange oaths and bearded like the pard,
> Jealous in honour, sudden and quick in quarrel,
> Seeking the bubble reputation
> Even in the cannon's mouth. And then the justice,
> In fair round belly with good capon lined,
> With eyes severe and beard of formal cut,
> Full of wise saws and modern instances;
> And so he plays his part. The sixth age shifts
> Into the lean and slipper'd pantaloon,
> With spectacles on nose and pouch on side,
> His youthful hose, well saved, a world too wide
> For his shrunk shank; and his big manly voice,
> Turning again toward childish treble, pipes
> And whistles in his sound. Last scene of all,
> That ends this strange eventful history,
> Is second childishness and mere oblivion,
> Sans teeth, sans eyes, sans taste, sans everything.

Jaques – *As You like It*

You may prefer to pick up on a trick of language. Here Romeo gives us a quick display of wit by reeling off a string of Petrarch-influenced oxymorons. He follows it with a definition of love. Both can be 'translated'.

> ROMEO   Alas, that love, whose view is muffled still,
> Should, without eyes, see pathways to his will!
> Where shall we dine? O me! What fray was here?
> Yet tell me not, for I have heard it all.
> Here's much to do with hate, but more with love.
> Why, then, O brawling love! O loving hate!

O any thing, of nothing first create!
O heavy lightness! serious vanity!
Mis-shapen chaos of well-seeming forms!
Feather of lead, bright smoke, cold fire, sick health!
Still-waking sleep, that is not what it is!
This love feel I, that feel no love in this.
Dost thou not laugh?

BENVOLIO   No, coz, I rather weep.

ROMEO   Good heart, at what?

BENVOLIO   At thy good heart's oppression.

ROMEO   Why, such is love's transgression. .
Griefs of mine own lie heavy in my breast,
Which thou wilt propagate, to have it prest
With more of thine: this love that thou hast shown
Doth add more grief to too much of mine own.
Love is a smoke raised with the fume of sighs;
Being purged, a fire sparkling in lovers' eyes;
Being vex'd a sea nourish'd with lovers' tears:
What is it else? a madness most discreet,
A choking gall and a preserving sweet.
Farewell, my coz.

Present writing transformed into a past style

This process is really very difficult. It requires intense close analysis and research. Do not expect fully authentic results! The attempt itself is enough, because there's a whole world of subtle discoveries to make, whether the outcome succeeds or fails. Nothing will expose the little tricks of word order and vocabulary of a past style more clearly than an attempt to reproduce it! It beats arm's-distance analysis every time.

To reduce the stress, and make the task more palatable, you may consider introducing humour – a parody or crude pastiche based on a specific style.

Texts that could be used for this transformation: Chaucer

Chaucer writes:

A knyght ther was, and that a worthy man,
That fro the tyme that he first bigan
To riden out, he loved chivalrie,
Trouthe and honour, fredom and curteisie.
Ful worthy was he in his lordes werre,
And therto hadde he riden, no man ferre,
As wel in cristendom as in hethenesse,
And evere honoured for his worthynesse.
etc.

Now how about a version as a parody, written in mock Chaucerian (to make it sound as authentic as possible)? What about:

> A chav ther was . . .

Texts that could be used for this transformation: Dickens

Dickens affords plenty of superbly 'copiable' passages, ripe for transformation. Here's the first description of Scrooge from *A Christmas Carol*:

> Oh! But he was a tight-fisted hand at the grind- stone, Scrooge! a squeezing, wrenching, grasping, scraping, clutching, covetous, old sinner! Hard and sharp as flint, from which no steel had ever struck out generous fire; secret, and self-contained, and solitary as an oyster. The cold within him froze his old features, nipped his pointed nose, shriveled his cheek, stiffened his gait; made his eyes red, his thin lips blue and spoke out shrewdly in his grating voice. A frosty rime was on his head, and on his eyebrows, and his wiry chin. He carried his own low temperature always about with him; he iced his office in the dogdays; and didn't thaw it one degree at Christmas.
>
> External heat and cold had little influence on Scrooge. No warmth could warm, no wintry weather chill him. No wind that blew was bitterer than he, no falling snow was more intent upon its purpose, no pelting rain less open to entreaty. Foul weather didn't know where to have him. The heaviest rain, and snow, and hail, and sleet, could boast of the advantage over him in only one respect. They often 'came down' handsomely, and Scrooge never did.

Students can borrow the structure of this passage to describe someone contemporary in Dickensian terms. Weaker students will simply change words, leaving the sentences largely intact. More able students may be brave enough to generate fresh sentences in the same style – exclamation marks, stacked adjectives and all.

Imagined future styles

What will happen to language in 200 years? What events in human history may intervene to influence the process? This is a fascinating speculation.

- Will texting become the norm? What will be the effects of abbreviation? Will the writing habits of online chat gradually infiltrate other written forms?
- Will there be some variation on Orwell's Newspeak, a simplified vocabulary?
- How will online social networking affect writing?

Perhaps one way to start might be to offer students a range of genuine writing types to translate – a newspaper article, an informal letter, an advert and a set of instructions – then ask them to imagine what the same piece would look like in a thousand years.

Some students might then want to write more at length.

If a large amount of novel vocabulary has been invented, students should supply a glossary (e.g. as Orwell does in *1984*).

Change of audience (different genders)

Here is a list of suggestions for activities based on this transformation:

- Article written for women, rewritten for men.
- Article written for men, rewritten for women.

What are the distinctive features of gender-specific writing? To change a piece from one form to the other, students will need to research and learn the distinctive elements of writing intended exclusively for women, and writing intended for men.

Is it possible to transform the intended audience with subtle alterations of vocabulary, or will large-scale changes of content also be required?

Texts that could be used for this transformation

- The transformation of a passage of a teenage girl's fiction to something that will appeal to boys
- The transformation of a non-fiction text

Try using a passage from *Girl, 15: Charming but Insane* by Sue Limb, published by Bloomsbury.

You could tell your class that it is clearly written for one gender. How can they tell? What are the clues? Ask them to transform the passage to be unambiguously aimed at the other gender. I recommend this method:

Working in pairs (and it may help to have a boy/girl team here!) do the following:

- Make two copies of the passage.
- Use your word processor's highlighter tool to mark one of the texts – yellow for words and phrases that will need to be changed; pink for sections that would be just impossible if the writing was aimed at the other sex, blue where you don't need to change anything; green where you may need to write something entirely new.
- Make all your changes.
- Compare your new version with the original and think about your changes – how much changing did you have to do? Were you forced into a complete rewrite or were you able to get away with simply changing words?

• Try your new version on another pair and see if they agree that you've succeeded in swapping the intended audience. Do they discover anything you have missed?

Change purpose

Here is a list of suggestions for activities based on this transformation:

- Serious writing transformed into satire or parody. Try a poem by Wordsworth.
- Description of a house designed to sell it, rewritten as the buyer's surveyor's report.
- Impartial information about HIV and AIDS rewritten as moral sermon against promiscuity.
- Bald statistical statements rewritten to form an argument.
- Satire or parody transformed into serious writing. Try Swift.

Here the attention falls on the audience and the inner workings of the text, its mode and tenor. Students examine the text given them on the screen and work on the key elements that determine its impact and purpose, changing the way it works for the reader. The outcome is a greatly enhanced understanding of how text work, what words in particular steer the text. Sometimes simply changing one or two words profoundly alters the purpose of the text.

Setting about changing the purpose of a text is perhaps the most overtly subversive of the 13 transformations – there's a strong temptation for mischief, a wicked realization of the power of the pen. It's equivalent to Duchamp's moustachioed Mona Lisa – a few strokes of a felt-tip and the picture is transformed from total seriousness to humour and iconoclasm! Personally, I would allow students to give vent to this verbal naughtiness – without permitting extremes of course. It gives writers a renewed sense of their own ability to shape the world of words. Besides, the practice is time-honoured and profoundly enjoyable. So perhaps start with parody. The word processor facilitates verbal tinkering and makes it easy to send up a sedate original.

Google will happily supply you with plenty of classical poems ripe for plunder. Go for famous, everybody-knows-this-poem examples. Classic Wordsworth, Kipling, even a Shakespeare sonnet. Save the texts in a shared area of the network or learning platform so that students can gain access to them.

A good way to launch the parody lesson is to project the image of a beautiful face with a toothy grin (a smiling model or film star, perhaps). Using the black interactive whiteboard pen, ask the class the following question: if they were required to transform the entire picture with one dot, where would they place it? Debate and experiment. (Placing a black dot on one white tooth is probably the most radical change of image). Explain that this is how parody can work; a subtle change in wording transforms the reading of the text.

Change tense

Some suggestions for activities based on this transformation:

- Experiment with the present tense – see what it does to the feel of the writing (examine examples)
- Experiment with future tense
- Try modal tenses. What do they do? (see *Sons and Lovers*, Chapter 2, which you can find at http://bit.ly/te_25). For example: 'Later, when the time for the baby grew nearer, he would bustle round in his slovenly fashion, poking out the ashes, rubbing the fireplace, sweeping the house before he went to work. Then, feeling very self-righteous, he went upstairs'.

This transformation is relatively simple to set up. Select a prose passage – especially one that focuses on action, with prominent action verbs. It should be written in classic past tense.

Display the text using a projector and as a whole class, identify the verbs – main verbs and auxiliaries.

With the class working in groups of two or three, set the task of transforming the text from past to present tense. When all the groups have finished (it shouldn't take too long) read out the original and the transformed version, and ask each group to comment on the effect.

Repeat, this time specifying future tense. What's the effect now?

Why might an author choose to write in the present tense (there are several contemporary examples)? What about future tense?

Texts that could be used for this transformation

Michael Frayn writes his novel *Spies* (2001) in the **present** tense – though it's full of memories. Identify an extract from the book – the opening paragraphs are ideal. Map the present tense verbs in yellow, the past tense in blue, for example: 'I *look* up at the sky, the one feature of every landscape and town-scape that *endures* from generation to generation and century to century'.

Transform the text by changing all the *present* tenses to **past** ones. What will you do with the verbs that are already in the past? Is there a past-past tense? Or will the past tense used by the author still work?

Transform the text again by making all the *present* verbs into **future** verbs. Can you do it? Is it nonsense?

Change one verbal element or word class

Here is a list of suggestions for activities based on this transformation:

- Nouns: experiment with power nouns – choose between a range of alternatives, between generic and specific nouns
- Nouns: examine how lists work in writing
- Proper nouns: investigate the effect of accumulated proper nouns
- Adjectives: see their effect on surrounding text
- Adverbs: how do they modify verbs and adjectives?

Experimenting with one grammatical element can lead to a fuller under-standing of the part it plays in shaping the impact of a text. The word processor allows you to skip through a piece and very swiftly identify and alter selected words. Allied to a study of effects used by professional writers this sort of exercise can be invaluable in helping to improve style. Students will become aware of these effects and it boosts their appreciation of literature: the relative power of individual words can be discussed, their impact and associations explored.

Using word-processor-based text-mapping, a teacher can mark (or ask students to mark) the targeted words so that they stand out – there's more about this in Chapter 3. Their effects in context are then discussed. After that, move on to discussing substitutions for the original words, noting the immediate impact of the new words. Sometimes it's subversion, often it seems like distortion; occasionally there's an improvement – and frequently substituted words weaken the original. Crucially, however, whatever the change, pupils learn by experimenting – and what they learn can be carried over to their own writing.

The exercise can be approached through cloze-type exercises, or as a variation on cloze, through preparing a version before the class where you have substituted patently inadequate words for the target class of words (e.g. the word 'nice' for very adjective).

Texts that could be used for this transformation

> Read the following verse of poetry. Where the poet used an adjective, another word has been used instead (marked in bold print). Work through the verse choosing altern-ative words of your own for these adjectives. Be careful – you may need to choose words with the right number of syllables and rhythm to make the line work properly.
>
> Season of mists and **damp** fruitfulness!
> **Nice** bosom-friend of the **old** sun;
>
>

> Conspiring with him how to load and bless
> With fruit the vines that round the thatch-eaves run;
> To bend with apples the **nice** cottage-trees,
> And fill all fruit with ripeness to the core;
> To swell the gourd, and plump the hazel shells
> With a **nice** kernel; to set budding more,
> And still more, **nice** flowers for the bees,
> Until they think **nice** days will never cease,
> For Summer has o'erbrimmed their **damp** cells.
>
> When you're satisfied with your version, you can compare it to the original, but don't cheat, or it will spoil your work. Why did the poet choose the words he did? Can you explain each one?

Change the narrative perspective or viewpoint

Here is a list of suggestions for activities based on this transformation:

- Rewrite from the viewpoint of another character
- Swap gender of the main protagonist (try a typical romance scene of the sort you get in Mills and Boone, a famous story, a biblical parable, folk tale or ballad). What other things need to be changed to make a gender-swap work?
- If the text is written in the first person, experiment with changing it to third. What is lost and what is gained?
- If the text is written in the third person, experiment with changing it to first. What is lost and what is gained?
- Try changing to second person – familiar to anyone?
- What does using first person plural do to our sense of the text?

Applied to strongly gender-biased texts, the 'swap-gender' exercise can be surprising in what it reveals about some of the underlying assumptions of language.

When we encourage developing writers to experiment with different narrative perspectives, allowing them to feel the effects directly in simple transformations like this can assist their understanding of the process.

The trick is very neat because the amount of editing is very light, but the transformation is radical in its effect.

You may wish to try using Find and Replace for a swift transformation.

- Select all the story by dragging your mouse over it
- Go to Edit/Replace – you will see a box appear on screen

- In the top box, type the first original word
- Click on the More button which can be found along the bottom of the box
- Click in the Find Whole Words Only box
- In the bottom box, type the appropriate transformation word
- Press Replace All
- Work your way progressively through the whole list until you've changed all the original words to the transformation words

Now you've got the basic work done, you'll need to go back and fine-tune the story so that it works. Change whatever you think needs changing.

Change by shortening

Here is a list of suggestions for activities based on this transformation:

- Condense copious notes into a haiku of three lines.
- Boil down flowery prose into a much-reduced poem.
- Work on a wordy poem to reduce the word-count.
- Trim down a long news article to fit an editor's restricted specifications without losing information.
- Read a persuasive article such as an editorial, and extract bullet points.
- Cut a play (or scene from a play) down to the bare essentials without losing the gist (scene from Shakespeare). This is an excellent task in that it relates to the rea cutting of plays being prepared for the stage, and provides us with an immediately accessible activity when you have large quantities of text in electronic form – the whole 'works', for instance.
- Work on text experimentally. Create a prototype text on screen. Remove some verbs. Cut back unnecessary words. How far can you go before the integrity and readability of the text is undermined?

Summary, concision, directness – these are admirable skills to encourage. A word processor takes the pain out of the process, and incidentally can count the number of words for you in a fraction of a second.

The last example can be used to discuss how far one can go with pruning a text before it becomes rhythmically awkward and as ugly as a hacked-back hedge. Do we gain on impact as we lose some of the verbal music?

Example:
From: *It was dark and the roaring wind made her shiver violently as she stood waiting for the bus. (18 words)*
To: *Darkness and roaring wind. No bus. She shivered violently. (9 words)*

Of course you can use the delete key to eliminate words in a piecemeal way. If you'd like to try a more wholesale deletion method you can use the high-lighter tool.

- Click on the highlighter tool (your cursor will change to a highlighter icon when you hover over the text).
- Highlight the text you want to keep by dragging over sentences and double-clicking on a word to select it.
- Go to Edit/Replace.
- Click on the More button at the bottom of the box to expand the Replace menus.
- Click in the top, 'Find what' slot.
- Click on the Format menu at the bottom of box and select Highlight. The word 'Highlight' will appear just under the slot.
- Click on the Format menu A SECOND TIME and select Highlight again. The word 'Highlight' will change to 'Not Highlight'.
- Click in the bottom 'Replace with' slot and type a space by tapping on the space bar.
- Click on the 'Replace all' button.

This routine swiftly deletes text and avoids lengthy and tedious use of the delete key.

If, instead of typing a space in the instructions noted earlier you type ^p instead (the ^ character can be found above the 6 on the keyboard) you will put each chunk of highlighted text on a line of its own – instant 'poetry'. You can also make the 'Replace' routine centre the text for you. Click in the bottom slot. Go to the Format menu again and this time choose 'Paragraph'. Click on the down arrow next to the 'Alignment' box and select 'Centered' (note American spelling). The word 'Centered' will appear under the bottom slot.

Texts that could be used for this transformation

The text (a wine review copied from the website Love That Wine) highlighted as described earlier:

I tried the 97 at a wine tasting a long time ago, and it was a truly outstanding wine. In fact it was the first outstanding wine I had tasted from Chile. Moving on to the 2003, whilst not outstanding it is excellent. It is more like a turbocharged Northern Rhone Syrah than an Aussie Shiraz. Suffice to say it has complex and huge aromas of white peppers, minerals, black fruits, mulberries and cloves. Its aromas are akin to a spice rack! Its palate is medium to full bodied, with a brawny

and tannic middle moving onto a muscular and long, powerful finish. This is
excellent value with the 3 for 2 deal.

© Love That Wine 2007

The unhighlighted text replaced with ^p and centred, and a suitable title and
ending added:

On drinking a glass of Chilean wine
turbocharged
complex
white peppers
minerals
black fruits, mulberries
cloves
aromas
akin to a spice rack
brawny
muscular and long
ahhhh!

Voila! The sensory essence of the original text extracted from the background
'noise'!

- Is it effective?
- Does it do the job in this bald format?
- Do we need to add any more words to it?

The highlighting method will work with any text where deletion is on a
radical scale.

Change by expanding

Example:
- Starting with a set of bullet points, or notes, expand into full sentences and fill
  out the writing to compose a complete article

Creating the bullet points can be an extremely useful precursor to this writing
task – perhaps through the time-honoured process of brain-storming.

A word processor allows text to be moved around easily. Bullet points can
be ordered into categories or arguments, the structure of the expanded piece
explored in skeleton form before the flesh is put on it, so to speak. You can also

use the Slide Sorter View facility in PowerPoint to arrange thoughts. It's easy to drag sides into new orders, to copy and delete them – and all this is usefully legible on an interactive whiteboard. Interactive whiteboard software offers similar facilities to rearrange pages.

Change form

Here is a list of suggestions for activities based on this transformation:

- Nursery rhyme to short story
- Fairy story to newspaper article
- Newspaper article to fictional prose
- Fiction adapted to a play script (for radio?)
- Play script turned into fiction (exactly the origin of *Of Mice and Men*)
- Poetry to prose
- Prose to poetry

To achieve success with this sort of task requires a thorough, explicit understanding of the stylistic features of the selected forms.

Change genre

Example:
- Cowboy fiction to Science Fiction
- Romance to crime etc.

Altering genre requires an understanding of complex rules and the ability to pick up subtle (or not-so-subtle!) verbal clues.

Change style

Here is a list of suggestions for activities based on this transformation:

- Formal Bible passage to an informal version aimed at young people, or formal Bible passage transformed to a narrative in the style of a novel (recent attempts at this transformation can be referred to)
- Highly descriptive flowery style to a plainer style and vice versa
- Formal passage translated into the vernacular and vice versa

Changing the style of a passage demands a degree of mastery over the language. It is a skill that all writers need to practise.

Conclusion

The transformations listed here are all immensely enhanced by the use of ICT:

- The text already exists in an electronic, adaptable form,
- Students get to grips immediately with the task itself, rather than spend time in mechanical operations like transcribing and physical cut and paste
- Editorial changes can be made and remade without excessive effort
- Global changes can be made to a text with the Replace function
- The shared screen allows local cooperation in editing and network connections allow extended forms of collaboration, between pupils, classes, schools and even between countries

And self-evidently, the activity itself employs the full range of English skills, with a stress on comprehension and writing, but also including speaking and listening.

6

Using ICT to Present and Perform

Presentation and performance are closely connected and often overlap. However, not all presentations are performances (readers will recall many INSET experiences where more of the latter would have enlivened the former) and not all performances are presentations. In this chapter we will consider presentations to have something specific to communicate, often with a particular audience in mind. Performances may be thought to be closer to pure entertainment, though frequently with an educational purpose or sub-text.

In a traditional classroom we would expect to experience presentations in the form of the class talk or the findings of some research augmented by visual aids, flip charts or posters. Performances would take the form of drama, poetry readings and so on.

The modern classroom still includes these elements but it also offers a greater range of possibilities. The key piece of equipment in this is the *digital* or *data-projector*, now a common if not standard piece of equipment and one which has in many schools revolutionized the teaching of English. Other ingredients in the form of equipment are the *interactive whiteboard* and the *visualizer*.

There is a wide range of software applications which are useful to present and perform:

- the widely available and probably pre-installed, for example, Microsoft products such as Word, MovieMaker and PowerPoint
- the freely downloadable, for example, PhotoStory 3 and Audacity
- that which needs to be purchased such as Serif Movie Plus

For most purposes in the teaching and learning of English, the simpler/more familiar programs are more than adequate.

Re-presenting written work

English teachers have always been suspicious of the use of word processors to type up fair copies of handwritten work, something which many pupils quite like as it gives the outward appearance of productive work while using a minimum of brainpower. On occasions this *can* be a necessary if mindless chore, perhaps when copy is required for a magazine or wall display and the original could only be written on paper.

Where the conversion of a previously produced text is a valuable activity, it tends to be something which gains in the process and requires the student to actively engage: to reflect and make choices. For example, the conversion of a story or piece of non-fiction writing into a slide show. Two examples follow.

Story to slide show

The class of 11–12-year-olds had already created their own story in a ghost/supernatural genre. Having enjoyed this activity, the teacher encouraged them when they wanted to 'illustrate' their stories and rather than add pencil and crayon or felt tip drawings to the handwritten texts, suggested converting the story to PowerPoint, adding illustrations along the way. Extra care was taken with spelling and punctuation as it was stressed that these versions would be shown to other classes.

Illustrations were created in whatever media the students could access at school or at home and then scanned. The resulting picture files could easily be imported into PowerPoint. The completed stories were a source of pride to the students and had the effect of motivating other classes to do the same.

Try this

Involve the art department so that students create their illustrations in the Art room. If the finished pictures are too large to be placed on the scanner, they can always be photographed instead.

If writing a non-fiction piece, for example a report based on research, use illustrations downloaded from the internet using an image search engine.

When searching for images using Google, make use of Advanced Image Search and select the option of images with a size over 1024 by 768. This will ensure that when they are displayed they will be of good quality and not pixelated – or blurred as we used to say.

Story to PhotoStory

Another example will serve to demonstrate the flexibility of these kinds of approaches. In this approach, students create their story collaboratively, with the teacher playing the role of guide, stimulator and scribe. Ideas are generated together and a general storyline agreed. Students then write their own first few paragraphs. These are shared in groups and the 'best' ideas then relayed to the whole class with teacher or reliable student typist creating the story using a word processor and a projector. The process is then repeated and the story gradually grows. Sometimes I have collected the class's writing and culled elements from as many students as possible and then created the next few paragraphs – always making it clear that these are open for editing.

This may seem a slow process but in many ways that is the point. Students are sharing a creative process and learning that getting a piece of writing right, or improving it as much as they can, takes time. The process of negotiating sentence structure, adding or deleting adjectives or finding more appropriate verbs is a crucial one in their writing development and in this way can be modelled powerfully and interactively.

Once the story has been created, there are many options. One is to use Microsoft **PhotoStory**. The process is as follows:

- Each student takes a paragraph and produces an illustration. These are scanned or photographed.
- The pictures are imported into the program and arranged in the correct sequence.
- Each paragraph of the story is then narrated by the illustrator and recorded, accompanying the picture.

- If required, transitions between pictures are customized, along with other pre-sentational features.
- Add a title and final credits.
- Add a musical background from a wide selection of pre-recorded music.
- Save the project as a media file.

The result is a professional looking slide show with all the appearances of a film. Along the way, students have also learned to speak clearly with appropriate pace and volume, deleting and starting again wherever necessary. Other members of the class or group usually appreciate the need to remain silent during recording but it's wise to take plenty of breaks between recording different sections and not to try to complete the whole thing in one session.

Voice over

In an age where communication is frequently thought of as giving primacy to the visual, we often forget how powerful sound alone can be. Radio did not die with the advent of television and is still enormously popular. As a means of presentation, *podcasts*, or simple voice recordings are very effective.

All computers have a basic sound recorder built in (see Chapter 1, 'Using ICT to Explore and Investigate', and the section in Chapter 3 on podcasting) so your laptop or desktop can be used as a tape recorder. What you may need to add are loudspeakers and microphones, unless your classroom is already equipped with them. Small powerful speakers are now widely available and cheap – the sort of thing you might buy yourself if the school won't. Headphones and mikes are not expensive either and it's worth having a few of your own tucked away in a drawer. Don't be persuaded that you need expensive equipment: you are not creating studio quality material and most of it you will not keep beyond the end of term.

Recorded responses make a useful alternative to written ones for many students and, in terms of literacy, are as valuable. A recorded response can also be a useful preparation for a written answer. Having gained confidence and organized thoughts verbally, some students will be better prepared and more willing to commit their thoughts to paper.

You might ask students which they prefer to do. Some will be happy to record their responses as long as you, the teacher, are the only audience. Most children will arrive in secondary education with experience of speaking in front of the class. If this is built upon as a matter of course and voice (and video) recording made part of the normal English experience, they will not be subject to the teenage shyness which can inhibit all sorts of work in their later school years.

The arrangement of your classroom and adjoining areas will affect the extent to which voice recording is feasible as an individual or small group activity. Headphones will prevent the playback disturbing others but there is no way of making the recording of voices inaudible to others – or, more importantly, preventing other noises being picked up by the students' microphones. The cheap microphones I have used are better in this respect in that they pick up sound from a smaller area. Uni-directional microphones and mikes built into headsets are also possibilities you may like to explore.

Students, then, may present their work in a sound recorded format if appropriate. Some may even prefer to record their homework. There is no reason why a response to a text should not take this form just as it might on a radio review, for example.

You may want presentations to be more formal than this, however. A group may decide to write and then record, for example:

- their answers to a set of comprehension questions;
- bullet points for a piece of persuasive writing;
- five headings for a response to an essay question or an alternative scene to *Romeo and Juliet* Act 1 Scene 5 – though this last, of course, will be more of a performance – if you're still distinguishing between the two.

An example of where presentation merges into performance can be seen in the work undertaken as part of a poetry project. Here students were given poems from the poetry anthology issued by the examining body and asked to record them in what they considered to be the most appropriate way. The results were played to the whole group for discussion. Along the way, students were encouraged to mark up the text with pauses, emphases, changes of voice and so on, which developed their attention to detail and encouraged their close reading. The full report 'Analysing the language of poetry through *podcasts*' can be found at www.nate.org.uk/htt and via the Continuum website.

Performance: Podcasts and radio programmes

We move unambiguously into the area of performance when sound recordings are to be made available to an audience, especially if that audience is the whole school. In the example I have in mind, a school engaged in a BSF (Building Schools for the Future) project incorporated a modern public address into the design. Rather than merely use it for office messages and demands for the Assistant Head to see Student Z at break time, the plan was to create a student radio station which would broadcast during morning and midday breaks.

Initially the English Department took charge of the project, which involved students aged 13–14 creating five minute **podcasts** on a range of subjects. These were suggested by students but vetted by teachers and ranged from fashion and pop music to interviews with people inside and outside the school. Some visited the building site (closely supervized!) and interviewed the contractors, and others interviewed parents who had attended the same school. These are now being edited and stored for use when the station goes live.

It's hard to think of a better activity which focuses on planning, research, scripting, questioning, speaking and listening – and all for a very clear purpose and a known audience. Inexpensive voice recorders were used and simple editing software such as Audacity. The plan is to create a leadership group from the students who will then be able to train other teachers and other students as well as acting as producers. The plan is to broaden the project so that it becomes truly cross-curricular, though in the process it will lose none of its relevance to English objectives. In addition, the boost to social and emotional aspects of learning is enormous.

Trip recorder

School visits are a rich source of material for English work and a powerful stimulus too. Their value can be enhanced if students are equipped with cameras – either still or video. The former are not only cheaper but the output is easier to manage.

In a trip to the local art centre and gallery, students were encouraged to take photographs of anything that interested them. That could be the lady behind the till in the café or the drain outside the building as well as any of the exhibits. While downloading them onto computers, they were asked to select just ten and give them suitable, clear captions – in other words, rename them from PIC001 to Drain-cover, for example. These were then copied into a common folder. The teacher showed the class the complete class set of pictures as a slide show and then managed a discussion of how they might best be organized to fulfil a particular purpose for a particular audience, in this case to persuade other members of the same year group that the visit was worth making in their own time.

Each pair was then charged with selecting no more than 20 pictures to be used as part of a PowerPoint presentation. A slide could consist of text only, text and picture or picture only and there was a limit on the number of words to be used on any one slide. The combination of selection and organization with a specific persuasive purpose in mind provided an ideal focus for English teaching and learning.

Image editing

In the example given, photographs were not edited. An extension to this activity would be to demonstrate the use of one particular form of editing: the *cropping* tool. This can be found in any picture management software, usually with this symbol.

As a fall-back position, insert a photograph into a Word document and click on it. A toolbar should appear offering the crop tool. If it does not, find the appropriate Toolbar menu and select Picture Toolbar. You will find the same tool in Windows Picture Manager.

The crop tool can then be used to demonstrate the effectiveness of removing parts of a picture and highlighting others.

Is this a political poster or a student T-shirt? What else might it be?

If we look at more of the picture we would probably revise our ideas slightly.

And if we see the complete picture we would revise them even more, showing as it does a sedate suburban roundabout.

Further work of this kind can be found on the Global Education area attached to NATE's website (/www.nate.org.uk/globed/). Select 'Images' from the left-hand column and you will find several lesson activities relevant to this type of work, especially the *Jigsaw Picture Activity*. Students will also enjoy searching out pictures which can be used in this sort of activity.

The effects of selection/cropping will soon become obvious and work in this area can be extended into news analysis, film studies and analogous critiques of written texts. What we leave out of a piece of writing (factual or fictional) is as important as what we include. This could lead on to an activity in transformation, where students take a piece of negative description and edit it to produce one which is either neutral or positive.

Try this

Using **Google Images** or a similar image search engine, students research an area of the country, either self-chosen or drawn at random. Their task is to produce two presentations of the same area, using the same photographs but cropped differently. One will show the area in a negative way, one positive, simply through the use of selective cropping and use of captions.

   To shorten or simplify this activity, provide students with a selection of pictures beforehand.

   See also the Picture Wall technique discussed in Chapter 1, 'Using ICT to Explore and Investigate'.

Research and development

Carrying out research and writing up a research report are higher level skills than we sometimes acknowledge. The former can deteriorate into a cut and paste exercise with gobbets of information – undigested – from internet searches represented as findings. While ICT has not caused this problem (it used to happen where students copied out verbatim chunks from whatever text they thought appropriate) it has exacerbated it. Students do need to be reminded that books still exist, often prove more reliable and sometimes present information in a better, more comprehensible way.

It's a good idea to always insist on a cross check. In other words, if one student is researching a particular topic, another student should be set the same task and the two need to agree to use information from different websites – and to cite them.

Once research has been carried out, though, presentation software provides a good way of helping students to focus and to organize. A PowerPoint presentation forces users to restrict themselves to a small amount of text per slide and to organize those slides into a coherent sequence.

Set a maximum number of words per slide – or a minimum font size – and ban long paragraphs. Encourage bullet points and numbering. This may seem counter to the instructions you normally give about writing; it's worth explaining to students that the purpose here is not a piece of continuous prose but a *presentation*. It needs to make a series of clear, well-organized points about the topic in question. It can then become the springboard for a piece of continuous prose both for the original researcher or the audience.

You may choose to use a different format for the presentation but whatever form it takes it still serves as a *motivator* (people are going to see it; it's quite fun to use) and a *tool* (it both forces you and helps you to sequence information or ideas). By the time students reach secondary education they should have overcome the need to try every font, colour and special effect but if they have not, insist that these aspects are tried out *after* the content has been created.

The green screen

A development of this approach is to move the research outcomes from written text (possibly accompanied with still images) to a full blown film. This may seem a giant step to English teachers not involved with media studies but can be achieved with relatively modest equipment and technical expertise. I have seen children aged 7–8 presenting their research on volcanoes, for example, using these means.

Clearly it is not difficult to put a camera in front of some students and record what they say and do. It doesn't necessarily have to be edited. To become a presentation or a performance, however, requires a good deal more work.

The Australia Project

Year 8 students (12–13 years old) were given a choice of topic and came up with Australia. The topic was broken down into smaller topics which were assigned (randomly) to small groups. Their task was to come up with a shooting script, the requirements of which were explained and demonstrated. If there had been more time, they would have practised with a trial run but as often this was a luxury which could not be afforded.

The usual problems and challenges of research were experienced but students were motivated and wanted to produce good film clips and knew that to do so they would need good scripts. Different genres were encouraged, including docu-drama, comedy, interview and expert-to-camera. Each resulting film had to include a minimum number of factual points and had to distinguish fact from opinion.

Students rehearsed and learnt some lines off by heart. Many brought in costumes and props of their own. The groups were then filmed against a 'green screen'. As it was not a play but a film, they could be prompted with their lines and could re-record those they fluffed or felt were not as good as they could be. Many aspects of speaking and listening improved, including clarity of speech and intonation – although not all students wished to be recorded and there was no insistence that they had to be.

After the filming, the resultant footage was edited, each becoming a three to five minute clip. The green screen technology then allows the green to be removed, leaving the actors against a plain background, rather as if they had been cut out from a sheet of paper. Any still or moving image can now be inserted with the result that the students appear to be in the desert, on the beach or in front of the Sydney Opera House. While this might seem to be a small advantage to simply filming them in the hall or the playground, the effect of the final product cannot be underestimated. The green screen technology allows students to produce a piece of work which looks professional and which both they and other students, not to mention staff, will want to watch. Take a look at this short video from Cleethorpes Academy as an example of what can be done: http://vimeo.com/14712854.

Now the caveats: equipment, space and time. You will need a room where you will be undisturbed and where the green screen and camera can be used for a reasonable amount of time – at least half a day at a time. You will need time to record your students' efforts (preferably while a friendly colleague is minding the rest of the class) and even more to edit them. And you will obviously need the hardware and software, though this can be shared with the whole school and the expertise to use them.

Many English teachers will see this as a hard to realize dream, those with media expertise less so. However, media savvy schools will appreciate the opportunities in terms of PR, liaison with parents and the wider community. As a school resource, it has much to recommend it. As a resource exploited by the English Department, the possibilities are endless: a scene from *Macbeth* with the rugged castle in the background, wind tugging at the trees, clouds building (free footage abounds on YouTube and elsewhere); news reports in a 'real' newsroom; book reviews with stills of author and book cover behind the reviewer . . . all these and more can then be archived and used as resources for the future.

Resource banks

A school resource bank can be built up from whatever recordings you are making. These don't have to be confined to English topics. The Department can make itself very popular by accepting commissions to produce clips for other subjects and/or offering itself for cross-curricular collaboration. Links with Modern Foreign Languages might be a particularly fruitful area to explore. Resources can then be stored on the school's learning platform (also known as **VLE**) assuming that it's up to the task.

Don't forget the aesthetics

Anything from a major school outing to a walk beyond the school gates can provide interesting photographs and while it may not be top of the Department's agenda to produce interesting and aesthetically engaging photographs, there are fascinating spin-offs for literacy too.

Consider these photos taken by students towards the top end of Primary (9–10 years).

The students proved to be very able to reflect on why they took the photos and then why they selected them from the wider collection. Aspects of content and style are discussed with little hesitation: choice of angle, depth, close up, cropping, colour, shade, juxtaposition (though they did not use that term) of images, ambiguity, the deliberate and the accidental . . . the list goes on. This kind of discussion provides a powerful experience to inform discussion of written texts, though the connections may have to be drawn out initially by the teacher. 'Do you remember when we were looking at those photographs you took.' It can give students a confidence in talking about aspects of their studies which can otherwise seem dauntingly abstract.

As well as intelligent discussion, the students in question went on to write well thought out and concise captions and gallery notes. Creating a title for a picture is an exercise in creative thinking as is writing a three or four sentence description for a third person to read. (What titles would *you* give to them?)

The requirements for this kind of activity are within the reach of almost all English Departments. *Digital cameras* are inexpensive and take photos of a quality quite good enough for enlarging to A4 or showing on a school display. Some come with a built in *USB connector* to download pictures straight onto a laptop or the school system; alternatively, you can usually take the memory card out of the camera and use the card slot already built in to many laptops or an inexpensive card reader. If school technology or photocopying/printing rules do not permit an in-school solution, resort to your local photo or copy shop.

A classroom display can be achieved quickly and relatively cheaply by taking the selected pictures on a flash drive memory stick to the shop where prints can be obtained for a few pence each. The prints can then be enlarged to A4 and printed in colour for an outlay of a few pounds for a dozen stunning images. I do this in two separate establishments, the photo developers and the local printers a few doors away and I still think it's magic.

7

Using ICT to Communicate and Collaborate

Chapter Outline

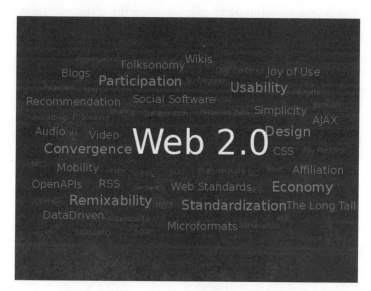

Web 2.0 is all about communication and collaboration.

Source: Original image by Markus Angermeier, vectorized by Luca Cremonini, from Wikimedia Commons: commons.wikimedia.org

In many respects, communication and collaboration are the culmination of activities described in earlier chapters. Many of those, of course, work best as collaborative activities, whether working on a presentation or making a short video. Students naturally enjoying working with their classmates – well, they usually do – and even though this can call for more active classroom management, teachers know that the most effective learning often takes place this way. ICT has for some time been promising to enable cooperation and user participation.

This is sometimes called 'Web 2.0' and encompasses social networking sites, podcasts and blogs, highlighting peer to peer relationships rather than the top-down ones from the early days of static web pages. The terminology isn't important; as the imminent death of Web 2.0 has been forecast for several years (the new dispute seems to be whether it will be succeeded by Web 3.0 or skip straight to version 4) we can concentrate on how technology can enhance and extend communication and collaboration in the real classroom. One palpable change is the way in which technology expands the classroom – or perhaps even dissolves its walls, so that we can not only talk about learning anywhere but also about collaborating anywhere too. An example of Web 2.0 applications that anyone can use is Google Documents (http://docs.google. com). Google Docs is not only a free online office suite, so that you can write and edit your documents from anywhere you have access to the internet, it also enables a group of authors to collaborate on the text at the same time – which is in fact how we created some sections of this book.

The opportunities for communication and collaboration include:

- mass access to information, both in school and outside school;
- communal participation in the construction and editing of text;
- publication and sharing of creative work, instantly, to a worldwide audience;
- flexible and dynamic forms of interaction and discussion across a range of distances;
- a variety of ways of sharing problems, solutions and ideas.

Other methods would simply not offer the ease and speed of communication that ICT now allows. While there is no substitute for a face-to-face meeting, we don't have the time or money to travel the globe to learn from students in other parts of the world but a simple audio or video link can allow us to exchange information and ideas and discuss issues – and in the process transform appreciation of the lives of others.

Easy access to information, at any time and from any place, is now taken for granted. It underpins many of the activities described in earlier chapters as well as some in this chapter – but it is only the starting point for learning. 'Looking it up' has to have a purpose; a collaborative activity can make finding a piece of information vital. As has been made clear earlier, students also need to be able to assess the accuracy of anything they find on the internet and detect any signs of bias. Here again, a focused task which students know will be subject to wide scrutiny offers a powerful incentive to get it right. If they know that their polemic on vegetarianism or recycling will be published on the school website rather than seen only by their teacher, they will know that they have to persuade a much wider audience. Teachers, for all our desire to encourage debate, can't be drawn too deeply into discussion of controversial issues (if only because of the lack of time) but if students present a sufficiently interesting and challenging case their peers in school and in other schools will certainly take advantage of any opportunities for feedback. The huge popularity of social networking sites with young people is testimony to this.

Blogging to boost writing

The widespread adoption of blogging was one the early manifestations of Web 2.0. Blogs enable instantaneous publication on the internet. Writers no longer needed to grapple with the technicalities and could just concentrate on creating content – which of course can include words, still and moving pictures, links and more. There are now millions of blogs; some have made their authors rich and famous, most languish unread. For English teaching, blogs provide students the means of publication for work that might otherwise have been confined to their exercise books, or at best been displayed in a classroom or found its way into a photocopied newsletter or magazine. A blog offers a potential audience which as well as the teacher and the rest of the class can include the whole school, parents and even (if you wish) the whole world. And this is an audience that has the ability to respond just a quickly as the writer can publish. Blogging still tends to focus on the individual writer (though of course there could be a team of writers behind a blog) and it tends to be the writer who decides on the initial content. This means that blogs are less of a collaborative tool than wikis and discussion forums – but have considerable potential for encouraging writing. One way to learn about the potential is to try one of the free blog services for yourself. I use WordPress, (www.wordpress.org) on my own site and can recommend the software; there is a free service at http://wordpress.com. Blogger (www.blogger.com) is another very popular blogging service – these are easy to join and within a few minutes you can be writing your own journal.

Try this

Nothing beats first-hand experience when you are going to try an activity with students, so if the activities here sound interesting, set up your own blog either on your institution's learning platform or virtual learning environment (if it offers this) or try one of the free sites such as Blogger, WordPress or EDU 2.0. You could use your blog to explain to students what they are going to do and why you want them to try blogging – and how you, too, are going to find out how it works. You'll learn how the system works, realize the potential – and also understand some of the challenges of managing this for a class of students.

In the NATE project on 'Making hard topics easier to teach with ICT', two teachers found that blogging provided powerful stimulus for some reluctant writers. Both independently found that the free EDU 2.0 for school service (www.edu20.org) provided what they required. Martin Brennan, teaching 15-year-olds on the English South Coast, had this list of key requirements: to create classes and passwords, to allow students to be anonymous, to make the blogs private and to delete anything inappropriate. As an EDU 2.0 administrator, the teacher has almost full control and each class is given a code. The site also includes wikis, chat rooms (useful but filtered sometimes by school networks), polls and blogs. Your school's learning platform may provide all these facilities, of course, though sometimes you need to ask the system administrator to make them available.

Martin found that once students began blogging, the ability to comment on other posts was a valuable opportunity for peer assessment. 'In the limited number of comments students made they were supportive if not incisive. But that is a skill we need to explore and this technology supports it brilliantly.' He also found that students had their own suggestions about managing their accounts, such as using their mobile phones to photograph their details and so avoid problems with forgotten passwords. Two students in particular became immersed in their blogs. Stacey, who had for two months refused to write in any lesson other than Science wrote three reviews on horror films and games. 'Not only that', Martin writes, 'she went on to write manga based fan-fiction and has opened a new world of literature to me. It turns out she reads this fiction obsessively . . . . Stacey's writing wasn't technically accurate, structured or incisive but I actually had writing, something I could work with. . . . When interviewed, Stacey said it was the ability to watch and write and continually refer back that engaged her. I think it was also in a medium she feels comfortable in: not pen and paper but online.' Another student was stimulated to write reviews of video games and then asked if he could blog his responses to the anthology they were studying for their examination. Martin concludes: 'The first thing you need from students to assess and improve writing is simply that: a text of theirs to work from. I now have these.'

A desire to provide his students with a real audience spurred Mark Ellis to use blogs. The week of work experience for the 15-year-olds in his Gloucestershire school provides unique material for reflection and comment. This overcomes one of the barriers to writing. 'But there is often a problem with the sense of audience', Mark adds. 'Just exactly who will be reading? Why will they be reading? How will they respond if I start like this? Or like this?' Using a blog was an effective way to address these issues and to provide an evolving account of events, with a preliminary post and a final reflective post after the week was over. One of the difficulties he faced was how to encourage students to point out technical errors in the writing of others without producing the smart that a public rebuke might cause. In the event, as he puts it, 'the advice to students that what goes around, comes around is easily understood' and students appreciated that if they expected considerate feedback they would need to be sensitive commentators themselves. Mark found that the sense of audience was markedly improved. This is best demonstrated in the opening sentences and the well-considered strategies that the students used. Here are a couple of examples:

> Yes I must admit I was there stood outside the doors of the Assembly rooms hopping from foot to foot. But I finally plucked up the courage and faced my fears of dealing with new people in a new environment.
>
> Well the end of work experience for me will be over in less than a couple of hours. But to be frank this hasn't been work experience for me. It's been life experience. I'm coming back from this placement a different person I know it sounds corny, but it's true.

Here are some sample comments from fellow students:

> I like the build up to the little boy booming (good use of booming much better than shouting) 'heroin' at the end of paragraph one.
>
> Yes. This needs a bit more work but what you've done here is good. The build up to the ending is quite effective, and really funny; the random things children come out with is certainly something you can use for humour's sake.

Mark concludes with some refreshing advice. 'You really have to get out of the way and let them do it. . . . This is an opportunity to save the red ink, and open up a different approach to the question of who should be taking responsibility for the accuracy of work.' You can read Mark and Martin's accounts of how they used blogs with their students in the area on the NATE site on 'Making hard topics easier to teach with ICT' at www. nate.org.uk/http.

Virtually partners

The ability to communicate with other students, even in another continent, opens up many possibilities. One simple yet telling example is illustrated by a short YouTube video entitled 'What does it mean to be American? British?' (http://bit.ly/te_7). A school in the English Midlands was exploring issues of culture. They had a contact in an American school who asked students there to create a short video answering the questions: 'What does it mean to be American?' and 'What does it mean to be British?' Of course the teenagers' descriptions of the English, complete with afternoon tea rituals, are amusing to British ears – but they demonstrate in a few seconds of video how others view us. The students' attempts to articulate what being American means to them seem even more revealing to outsiders. The fact that these students are able to speak with confidence about this issue should provide much material for discussion. There was a real audience in the partner school – and there is also the whole audience of YouTube visitors. It demonstrates that effective communication can take place using only a basic video camera and editing software – along with a well-focused question or two. Earlier chapters, particularly Chapters 1 and 3, have discussed podcasts and video recordings – linking with another school is a powerful way to lend a personal dimension to this kind of creation and publication. Many schools already have international links, and if not, sites such as Global Gateway from the

UK Department for Education (www.globalgateway.org.uk) provide ways of finding partners.

The AfriTwin project illustrates what is possible when schools make a serious commitment to international links – and how ICT can help. Jemma Defries summarizes the benefits of the links between her school in the Wirral in the UK and two in South Africa, which was set up under the auspices of AfriTwin (www.afritwin.net). 'An AfriTwin club is an asset to our school and a great opportunity for the pupils to learn about other cultures. It can open up new experiences for children on both sides of the world who may not necessarily have the funds to travel. It is a modern day pen-pal system that produces thought-provoking discussions.' As the schools developed the relationship, they found a number of interesting links that enabled a range of cross-curricular activities to take place. One was the *HMS Birkenhead* project; they discovered that in 1852 a boat that set sail from Birkenhead (not far from the English school) sank while transporting troops at Danger Point near Gansbaai on the outskirts of Cape Town, South Africa (near one of their partner schools). The Wirral pupils put together a dramatic re-enactment of the journey of the ship, filmed it and sent it to the partner school. It was also placed on the learning platform for parents and families to view. This gave pupils a common ground to work from and drove the project forward. They also worked together across three schools and their feeder primary schools to write their own International Student Council Charter. They filmed pupils from all schools making their pledge, which was edited and placed on the learning platform to share with all the schools involved.

An important aspect was the creation of a secure community. The advantage of the learning platform hosted at the English school was that it enabled Jemma to set up a secure blog that only the students involved could access; this kept students safe online and they liked the idea of belonging to an exclusive club. They also enjoyed having contact with more than just one person, in contrast to a traditional pen-pal. One pupil commented that it was 'more fun and less like hard work' when using the learning platform. Another said: 'I like the way I can potentially read about the lives of many pupils in South Africa. I have so many questions; it would be unfair to ask one person to answer them all!' Jemma adds: 'With technology developing all the time, blogging appears to be the best way to allow our pupils freedom of expression but in a very safe environment.' You can read her AfriTwin report on the learning platform project area of the NATE site at www.nate.org.uk/page/lp.

Wikis: working together – anywhere, any time

The value of wikis as a way of recording reactions and research has already been mentioned in Chapter 3, 'Using ICT to respond, interpret, reflect and evaluate'. A wiki is, essentially, a website that can be edited by users. For students, the advantage is that groups can create resources collectively, with everyone able to see the results instantly. Collaboration is the whole *raison d'etre* of wiki software, with its facilities to record all the changes made, who made them and when. It also provides the reassuring ability to revert to an earlier version if the authors decide to reject a later change. This can readily be demonstrated by looking at the structure of a Wikipedia page, with its record of edits. At the time of writing, for example, the Wikipedia page on the Pre-Raphaelite Brotherhood had the following entries at the top of the Discussion page: 'This sentence is rather unclear: . . .' followed by the reply from the original author: 'Yes, it's utter and complete gibberish. . . . Some idiot has rewritten it.' The View History section provides a record of the edits. (These features could also prove useful when studying the reliability and authenticity of online sources, as suggested in Chapter 3.)

Better still, students should gain experience of creating their own pages. A wiki page is blank; the project could be to provide information (advice to students joining the school, say), based on an issue (animal rights, for example) or the aim could be to create revision resources on set texts. There is often a discussion facility attached to wiki pages which enables students to comment on the content. Once students become engaged, discussion can be lively and it is interesting to see how students will often move away from the original focus to suggest independent approaches or questions.

School learning platforms or virtual learning environments (VLEs) usually include a wiki facility and there is other software that can be installed on an institutional intranet; if not there are free online versions such as Wikispaces, which offer private areas for education free of charge (www.wikispaces.com). The institutional option should normally be preferred, since not only should you be able to rely on security features established in accordance with your school or college's requirements rather than having to check these for yourself but students will already have user names and passwords so you won't have to set these up and cope with the problems when, inevitably, someone forgets.

Student contributions will also all be logged along with their other access to the system and linked to their other work in English to create a virtual portfolio of all their work. Don't be deterred, however, from trying out another service; students are used to having a number of online identities and may enjoy using a less official alternative. In some cases a short-lived project is all you need, especially since you can always capture the final product for the record, even if the online version is allowed to languish. You can find out more by visiting one of the popular wiki providers, such as EDU 2.0 for school (www. edu20.org) or Wikispaces (www.wikispaces.com; take the 'Tour' and see the special educational service in the 'K-12' area).

Editing a wiki page on Wikispaces.

One important aspect, whether using a provider such as Wikispaces or a learning platform, is the ability for students to contribute from wherever they have internet access. This means that work can continue from home (or from the library after school) and that those on school trips or away from school for a variety of other reasons can also be involved. Some schools have created curriculum projects in which students work off-site for a whole day carrying out research, conducting interviews and working in groups. It also means, as the AfriTwin project described above has shown, that schools in different countries can cooperate on projects. This involves careful planning, including the provision of facilities (either in school or at locations such as local libraries) for those without access at home, but also permits a whole range of activities and research as well as giving students a taste of independent study.

Chris Hirst, working in an inner-city Manchester school, describes one such activity in the NATE learning platform project (www.nate.org.uk/page/lp). All 164 of the school's 12- or 13-year-old students worked at home on a gun crime project and submitted the results to the school's learning platform, Moodle. Careful planning meant that parents and students were fully briefed and knew what to do if there were practical problems. Each task contained links to relevant reading material on the web, including newspaper articles, Wikipedia entries and YouTube clips. Teachers were able to see at a glance when each student completed a task and to provide feedback. One unexpected consequence was that some students wanted to respond to their teachers about this (a rare occurrence when work is marked in the traditional way on paper). One commented to the teacher: 'I'm glad you liked my presentation. You said that I didn't have enough pictures in it. I'm going to download some . . . and put those in then send it back to you.' Chris also found that students used the online chat facility which he had originally intended to disable as he thought they might become side-tracked. Some found this a great help, one reporting: 'One of my friends got stuck so he messaged me and I helped him out.'

Thinking it through

Select an activity that students can complete online, either in its entirety or combined with some classroom input and feedback. Aim to include at least some group work, such as collaborating on research or interviews.

- What kind of project will be most suitable for this approach?
- Will it involve online research, activities outside school such as interviews with members of the community or the creation of their own materials such as a class or group story or newspaper?
- How much will you need to provide in the form of ready-made information, links to resources, etc., and how much can you leave to the students' own initiative?
- Will you need to adapt existing materials or write new units, including online activities such as questionnaires, etc.?

⇨

Consider how normal classroom approaches will need to be modified when students are working remotely. How will you prepare them for this way of working? How will you supervize them during the activity? How can they seek help? How can you seek help – for example if access to the school network is problematic? What will you need to tell parents, colleagues and members of the school or college management?

You will realize that this way of working involves rethinking teaching and learning, although for English teachers used to encouraging group and project work the changes are likely to be more a matter of degree than a transformation.

Bringing it together

An experienced teacher knows how to employ a repertoire of skills and resources to meet the specific needs of his or her classes. Techniques and technology are used because they are appropriate, enhancing other methods or providing new opportunities. Teaching about language, for example, can be enriched by websites such as the BBC's Voices (www.bbc.co.uk/voices/) and the British Library's Sounds Familiar: Accents and Dialects of the UK (http://bit.ly/te_9) but such resources (though wonderful) need to be integrated within a teaching and learning programme. Louise Astbury's work with 18-year-olds illustrates a multi-strand approach by bringing together readily available tools. Her students used a combination of video resources, blogs and PowerPoint presentations to explore language samples as part of their study of language and power. Louise recorded a number of television programmes such as *The Weakest Link, Jo Frost Extreme Parental Guidance* and *Hell's Kitchen USA* for students to explore as part of their final examination preparation. Her college had access to a service called eStream, which stores recordings and splits them into easily annotated 'chapters' for students to select and annotate the features they observed – allowing them to collaborate in groups by accessing the videos from college or home (YouTube is a less sophisticated alternative). Her objectives were 'to allow students to develop their learning outside the classroom, to work collaboratively on analysing video and to allow them to become more independent and autonomous in their activities'. To this end they completed private learning journals which Louise could view and also recorded more public comments on a blog in which they could add images and YouTube clips as they prepared their group presentations on their chosen video extract.

In their learning journals, students focused on the fact that they were free to explore the data for themselves. One wrote:

> The fact that our teacher has had hardly any input has definitely benefited every-one as we are learning to be independent and not so reliant on the teachers for help or advice. We were forced to use our own initiative.

They liked the independence and other comments related to feeling more confident in expressing their ideas as they had time to think and process the material rather than being under pressure to respond in front of others in the classroom. In addition, everything was available on the learning platform, from the initial videos to the resulting blogs and presentations, which meant that they (and the others in the class) could return to these for revision. Louise concludes that the benefits were not confined to the students: 'Will this help them with the examination? Yes, in that they were responding to previously unseen data and had to apply and evaluate materials covered in class. The learning journals were important in allowing the students to reflect on not just what they were learning but how they were learning. These comments are also useful in informing my teaching for future classes in allowing them to be more autonomous in their learning.' You can read her full case study on the NATE site: www.nate.org.uk/page/lp.

Wiki wars

We mentioned in Chapter 3 the value of wikis and discussion forums when studying literature. Teachers of older students, in particular, face a number of competing requirements when students approach examinations. The students are expected to be familiar with the set texts, moving beyond merely knowing 'the story'; they need to be able to discuss and evaluate opinions and communicate a personal response, supporting their comments from the text. Small group discussion offers a way for students to develop their own ideas and a route to avoid the mere parroting of a prepared answer. Even in the best regulated classrooms, however, unless numbers are very small, it isn't possible to ensure groups stay on task, avoiding errors and misleading interpretations, and to ensure all students are able to contribute and receive feedback. This is an area where technology, in the form of forums and wikis, offers a real enhancement, giving students considerable autonomy while allowing the teacher to monitor all contributions. A couple of examples demonstrate the sometimes surprising ways students engage with these online activities.

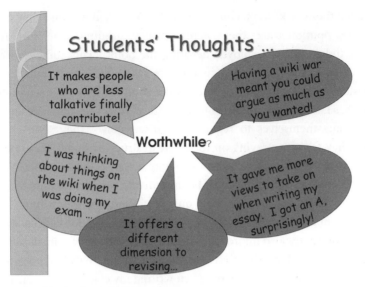

Students enjoy debating in a wiki forum.

Source: Image created by Carol Weale, used with permission from her case study for NATE: nate.org.uk/htt

Carol Weale was faced with the task of engaging 16-year-old students in the study of a poetry anthology, exploring the use of language, form and structure in a sustained manner. 'How', as Carol put it, 'do you elicit that personal response that has not come out of a carefully rehearsed answer?' Her answer was to create a student-led environment for stimulating and interesting discussion where they could explore each other's interpretations and use their familiarity with online discussions to engage their interest in posting responses. The result was that they really became involved in the creation of a literary community. What began as a project to create a series of wiki pages on the poems as an aid to revision took a dramatic turn when students discovered the power of the discussion feature on each page. Carol noticed a progression from what she termed 'worksheet language', where students answered the teacher's question in a rather formal and awkward register, to much more personal and engaged discussions as they became more confident:

> And finally Lydia, you said the mother is 'sad' because 'her daughter doesn't have such a need for her as she wishes,' which is wrong, the rope of love is red, signifying passion or hate (i.e. passionate hate), sadness is the colour of deep blue. I rest my case.

The discussions became more heated and Carol found that students became increasingly competitive and conducted up to four discussions simultaneously.

She called these 'wiki wars', commenting: 'When asked whether they actually held the opinion that they were strongly arguing, one girl replied that she didn't, but just enjoyed debating the point!' This combative aspect also seemed to draw in students who were reluctant to contribute to group discussion in class – and the debates would continue long after school hours, sometimes late into the night. As teacher, Carol learnt to step back and allow the students themselves to regulate the discussion – they soon chastised anyone they felt was straying off topic ('Yeah Bruce be quite! This poem has nothing to do with the slave trade – it's about a man killing his wife! Woo! Go me and Tanya'). 'So the quiet and the unmotivated suddenly came to life and the wiki was populated with their quips, wit and analysis without fear of censure from a teacher.' The effects went further: Carol found that students' examination scores also improved. This was on the basis of a small sample, of course, but the students themselves certainly felt the activity had helped them: 'It gave me more views to take on when writing my essay. I got an A, surprisingly!' and it was summed up by one boy, 'I think it should be for everyone as they would gain vast amount of different interpretations giving us a wider knowledge of the poems'.

Anna Richardson, whose work with slightly younger students in a Coventry school has already been described in Chapter 1, also found that involving students in creating wiki pages enabled them to become more independent learners. She sums up the benefits in ways that confirm Carol Weale's findings:

> Without doubt, the most useful tool is the discussion page. Some of the discussions going on between students of all abilities was, quite frankly, unbelievable. . . . Suddenly, it seemed there was no need for me!

One reason that the learning experiences were so powerful was that the use of the wiki had spread beyond one class; not only was she using it for two classes in the same year group but other teachers, fired by her enthusiasm, asked her to set them up with wikis. Her response was to ask her students to teach the teachers. She found that the students in different classes were helping each other, assisted by her decision to allow them to choose their own user names so that the shy ones could assume an alias, 'lessening any chance of ridicule', as she put it. Soon they were posing their own questions and connecting with the text in a more personal way: they were now beginning to see the poems as relevant to them. This was graphically illustrated when Stinky Potatoe Head [*sic*], having read what both Dickens and Carol Ann Duffy have to say about Miss Havisham, asked:

> If Miss Havisham were alive today, which celebrity wud she be best with?? hey, JOIN THE DISCUSSION! Lets hear what u think??

As you can imagine, other students rapidly contributed a lively list of celebrity names.

Anna and Carole's case studies from the project on 'Making hard topics easier to teach with ICT' can be read in full on the NATE site (www.nate.org.uk/htt).

Further approaches

By this stage, we hope that the advantages of using ICT to facilitate collaborative work will be clear. In this concluding section we'll explore more briefly a number of other activities where the technology will encourage more cooperative working.

Creating a multimodal accompaniment to live performance: Chapter 3 included a suggestion for 'PowerPoint counterpoint' in which students use the presentation software to build a multimedia background to a live performance – a scene from *Macbeth* was the example given. An extension of this would be to use simple video editing software such as that which comes free with Microsoft Windows or Apple's MacOS. This allows groups of students to assemble images and sounds into a short movie. They can use material gathered from the internet or create their own using a digital camera – even cheap still cameras now have basic movie capabilities and students will enjoy exploring these. Similarly, a simple microphone plugged into a laptop will allow them to record their own narration and create sound effects.

Communal participation in the construction and editing of text: This is a new presentation of an old idea, in which groups of students or even a whole class write a text together using the facilities of a wiki to collaborate. A story is the most obvious project, though it could just as easily be non-fiction – how about creating a guide for students coming to the school in the new academic year? If students are creating a narrative, how will you start it – with an opening sentence you provide? With an ending they have to work towards? Or both beginning and end, with the challenge to explain the story in between? Will you give them the middle? Or simply supply a list of objects, places and names?

Reviews: Everyone is familiar with readers' reviews on the Amazon site – you might explore one or two of those as examples first. Try to look at some sites aimed at young readers too, such as Cool-reads, created by Tim and Chris Cross (www.cool-reads.co.uk); although it is now archived, it should provide plenty of ideas and demonstrate the interest in sharing readers' views and the ways they have classified texts. Students can create their own review site using wiki or blog software; book covers can be included and of course several readers can contribute comments on each text if they wish. Why not ask students to record themselves reading short extracts too, to whet readers' appetites? You need not restrict this to books, of course – films, games and television can be given the same treatment.

Interact with writers: A visit from an author is a powerful stimulus but not always possible – and it's rare that schools can have the pleasure of a writer in residence. A 'writer in virtual residence' could be an interesting alternative, using email, a blog or video conferencing. If you don't have contact with a local author, try one of the national organizations such as Booktrust (www.book-trust.org.uk) and its Everybody Writes project (www.everybodywrites.org.uk), The National Association of Writers in Education (NAWE: www.nawe.co.uk), and NATE in the UK (www.nate.org.uk) or your equivalent national subject association for contacts.

Create a literature wiki about authors: This is another development of a traditional activity, in which students collaborate to create a rich resource about an author or authors they are reading. The complexity will depend on the age and abilities of your students. You might include historical and social context, character studies and hot-seating activities in which students take on the role of an author from the past – or one or more of their characters – and answer questions from the rest of the class. You could extend this to consider other treatments of the authors' texts such as films.

Exploring language: Students can be fascinated by language and all its quirks. A wiki to explore dialects could lead to them gathering sound recordings from the locality as well as from visitors from other parts of the country (and the world). They could also create a dictionary (or wiktionary) about newly coined words or to build up a useful glossary of terms encountered in their lessons, from allegory to zeugma.

Podcasting: This method of publishing students' recordings has already been described in Chapter 3. Podcasting is just another form of publishing so it can be used to accompany, or showcase, any of the projects in this chapter, involving as many students as desired. What about recording an interview with a writer (in school or remotely) along with some of the work students have written in response? This could be made available on the school website as a demonstration of the creative activities in school.

Simulations: In the early days of computers in schools a number of teachers created classroom simulations which made use of the single computer and printer which was often the extent of the facilities available. The computer would print out a news stream; scenarios ranged from investigating a road accident to a murder enquiry or full-scale emergency. These proved very powerful ways of involving large numbers of students with only limited resources; one simulation based on a Victorian mining disaster involved thousands of students in schools across a whole Midlands county for a day. The scale of these events and the fact that currently there are none readily available to use off the shelf makes them beyond the scope of this book. You might, however, be stimulated by what you have read here to create your own. What about linking up with the junior school that sends students to your school? You could devise a collaborative activity in which students communicate with each other online to solve a problem or resolve a situation. Could they work together to design improved play areas for your locality, for example?

Putting it into practice

The approaches outlined in this chapter ask students to work independently, recording the process and outcomes using online tools. We hope that you will have been stimulated to try one or more yourself. Select a topic in your own teaching where you can provide or direct students to a variety of resources, so that each group has its own material. These could be video clips, a set of images, newspaper articles, a collection of poems or a combination of all these. The topic could be literary, such as Gothic literature and why it remains popular today or an investigation of a controversial topic like designer babies or advertising and young people. The final presentation could be in presentation software such as PowerPoint, wiki pages, short videos or newspaper or magazine articles.

Don't be afraid to start in a modest way, perhaps with a single basic wiki page for each group. Involve your students in the setting up so that you can learn together – you will all learn faster that way. Establish straightforward rules so that students understand that any abuse of the system will result in sanctions such as being barred from the site (if you are using a wiki, you should receive a message each time a change is made and by whom, so you will have a clear record). Ensure that they all have access, in and out of school, to the system you are using. Students also need to understand how to call for help – and you will need to decide the extent to which you will monitor and comment on their work in progress. If possible, ask them to record their progress in a blog or journal.

Finally – have the confidence to step back and allow the students to take control!

8

Using ICT to Inspire and Engage

Inspiration is one of the key ingredients for creativity. Sometimes it has a short-term effect but it can also be the slow-burning fuel of artistic endeavours that last for years.

By contrast, *engagement* is short term – it's what holds the attention of a class during a lesson, with those unmistakeable on-task symptoms of focus, rapt listening and energetic responses to teacher instructions. Once a class is *engaged*, the process of teaching becomes one of steering rather than driving, guiding rather than motivating.

Inspiration and engagement are linked: one fosters the other.

In this regard, from their first introduction into classrooms as teaching tools, computers have been useful. They seemed to carry with them an immediate guarantee of engagement. A fractious, bored class suddenly became keen. The symptoms looked familiar too, with all the appearances of real engagement.

However, although the symptoms seem the same, we need to be quite critical of the apparent engagement afforded by ICT in the English classroom. We need to be able to discern the difference between enthusiasm for the technology (quite unrelated to the content of the activity) and real intellectual engagement with the content of the lesson.

A teacher can show a video to the class and achieve what looks like rapt attention; can use resources that feature multimodal effects – and again the students seem riveted; can introduce drag and drop activities to the interactive whiteboard or play with voting systems and see a rise in enthusiastic participation – but the technology cannot be a substitute for properly engaging *content*. One cannot think 'job done' just because children like technical gadgets.

'Inspiration' is a much tougher test for the use of ICT. You can think of engaging activities that involve computers – but do they 'inspire'? Did the video in fact induce an alpha-wave zombie state in the class rather than exciting intellectual responses? Were the multimodal effects simply pandering to the stimulation-hungry, short-attention-span mentality of some young people?

In this chapter we want to maintain a critical stance while suggesting some genuinely inspirational approaches. They have the advantage of ensuring engagement too.

How can ICT help to inspire and engage?

The trick, as implied in the introduction to this chapter, is to focus on the content and the activity rather than the technology. The aim should be to find applications that have the greatest intellectual impact – without the upstaging effect of distracting and ultimately irrelevant digital packaging.

This chapter will explore the use of **random function effects** applied to English – electronic 'dice throwing'. Since the introduction of computers to the classroom, it has proved to be a very fruitful source of novel approaches.

The first program for English that used random functions was a little activity designed by Anita Straker for the BBC 'B' machine, called Wordplay. You typed in four lists of words sorted by word class, specified the order that these classes would appear and then the program would generate random combinations of words to that recipe in the form of little 'poems'. If a word was misplaced (an adjective in the verb list, for instance) then it would sound wrong when it appeared – so you would go back to the source lists and edit away until the program produced valid results. Often what was produced had an unexpected quality, frequently delightful – surprising images generated by the accidental confrontation of word with word.

It's not a new idea, of course. English teachers (and before them countless parlour game players) have found consequence-type games entertaining – where a student writes a phrase on a piece of paper, folds the paper over and passes it round to the next student in the circle. (Indeed the Manchester Art Gallery's recent exhibition, *Angels of Anarchy, Women Artists and Surrealism*, featured a 1920s variation called 'The exquisite corpse' (*Cadavre Exquis*), derived from the parlour game 'Consequences'. The idea was to generate surreal, mind-challenging expressions.) The effect is to randomize the input, exactly parallel to Wordplay's routine, with hilarious results.

Using a computer to drive the activity has several advantages:

- Speed
- Richness of the input lists
- Ability to alter the input recipe easily, to change the pattern of words
- Ability to manipulate, edit and save the results
- Ability to print
- Ability to mark and map each word class with a coloured background

So there have been a number of experiments with random functions for English in school. A brief history of runs like this:

- Anita Straker's Wordplay
- Michael Green's StoryStarter Fruit Machine (produced by Actis)
- WordSpin (produced by Actis)
- Wordwhiz (produced by Teachit)

The StoryStarter Fruit Machine by Michael Green

This lovely activity involves several levels of random selection. The player is presented with the familiar four wheels of a classic fruit machine. Above the wheels there are four yellow buttons representing four story genres: Horror; Science Fiction; Real Life; Romance. A player can select or de-select these buttons to produce a story recipe. The ingredients can all come from one genre, or if a combination of genres is selected, the result is a random mixture. The four wheels represent four key components of a narrative:

Who (Main Character), Where (Location), Why (Quest or problem), What (Key Item).

When the big PLAY button is pressed, all the four wheels spin showing words instead of the little usual coloured symbols. If a player doesn't like the outcome, it is possible to spin the wheels again; Hold or Nudge one of the wheels. Finally the player clicks on Collect and the program produces the recipe.

This is an example of the Fruit Machine output, using a combination of Horror and Sci Fi:

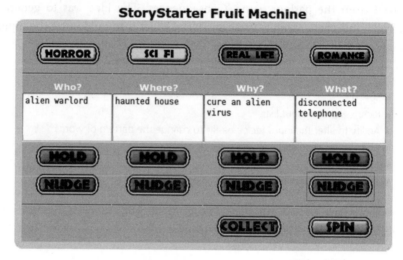

StoryStarter Fruit Machine

HORROR	SCI FI	REAL LIFE	ROMANCE
Who?	Where?	Why?	What?
alien warlord	haunted house	cure an alien virus	disconnected telephone
HOLD	HOLD	HOLD	HOLD
NUDGE	NUDGE	NUDGE	NUDGE
		COLLECT	SPIN

English Online from Pearson Ltd: englishonline.co.uk (by permission of Pearson Education).

Pressing Collect gives this story recipe:

Story starting point

Principal character of the story: **alien warlord**
Will this be the hero or villain? Will they narrate the story, in a first person narrative?

Main location of the story: **haunted house**
Will the story begin or end here? Will there be other locations?

The main problem that has to be solved in the story: to **cure an alien virus**
Are there other problems to solve? Will it be solved at the end, to create closure in your story?

Key item in the solution to this problem: **disconnected telephone**
Will this be a help or a hindrance? Is it something that has to be found?

When I first saw Michael's application I was amused and felt drawn to play with the combinations, but I felt privately that it was a bit trivial. I had no idea how powerful this little program was until I tried it out in a live lesson on a hot Saturday afternoon in Runcorn City Learning Centre. I was down to lead a creative writing session with a group of Gifted and Talented pupils. Outside their peers were happily playing football, and the group were tired and bored – counting down the minutes until the day ended. I launched the Fruit Machine activity and to my delight it gripped them. The task was simple – working in pairs, create a story formula and begin to write it. Remarkably the initial engagement transmuted into genuine inspiration. When the official time was up and I said they could go, there was universal unwillingness to stop, and a determination to finish the work at home. You can see (and play) a demonstration version of the StoryStarter Fruit Machine here: http://bit.ly/te_3.

Why do such activities achieve this effect? I believe it is partly the puzzle effect. If we are presented with a range of random elements, and challenged to combine them into a coherent story, we find ourselves engaged in the whole process of narrative construction. Instead of the daunting blank sheet we have a scaffold to work on. The actual input from the computer is minimal – the effect is to generate maximum mental and intellectual activity. Contrast this with the sensory bombardment of some multimedia programs and the comparatively poor creative activity they generate. There's a lesson to be learnt here! Restraining technology can give the human brain better space to work – less is more. Don't allow computers to usurp the role of the mind or do the intellectual work for a class.

Teachit's *Wordwhiz*

This Flash application is available to Teachit subscribers. To drive the program, you drag a set of tiles along the bottom of the screen onto the working area and arrange them into a suitable pattern, the empty template of a sentence or poem. When you press the Whiz button, the program flips to the play screen, selecting random words or phrases from its lists for each tile. If the original pattern makes grammatical sense, the resultant text will read grammatically too – though the sense may be ridiculous or illogical. Clicking Edit takes you back to the pattern-forming screen so you can readjust the sentence template at will.

At the very least it is a marvellous way of allowing students to 'play' with grammatical structures in an experimental fashion. In so doing, word classes that have been learnt as definitions ('a noun is a naming word') begin to be part of a language logic – they start to make sense.

The ability to form *any* template also means that there isn't a limit to the final form of the random sentence – it's a much more flexible format than Wordplay. Wordwhiz allows you to copy the output to a word processor for final editing.

There are four variations to play with (the current version does not give user-access to the word lists that drive the program):

- Insult Whiz
- Weird Whiz
- Haiku Whiz
- Title Whiz.

Insult Whiz is loaded with a compilation of Shakespeare's most insulting vocabulary. As mentioned earlier you can form any template you like from the components – if you want to you can use six or seven adjectives in front of the noun; you can try adjectives on their own; you can build a crescendo of insult, or inject a stinging 'last word':

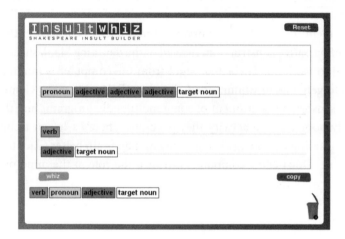

Pressing the orange 'Whiz' button generates the randomized utterance:

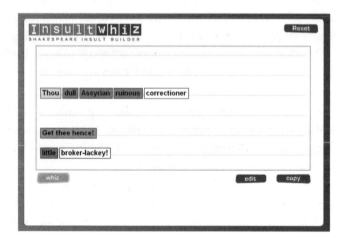

Press Whiz again for a completely new insult. Click 'edit' to change the template.

Haiku Whiz

Here's Teachit's Haiku Whiz. This takes the whole game up to its ultimate expression – not only do you have to arrange the word classes to make sense, you also have to count syllables (a haiku is 5, 7, 5).

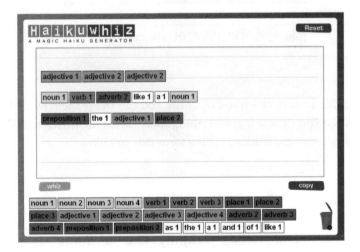

The results are frequently bizarre, but often surprisingly lyrical.

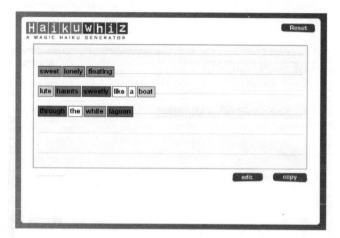

The word classes are colour-coded, so you can see their position and influence.

If you like a word, or a series of words, you can freeze them by clicking on them. When you click Whiz, everything spins except the frozen words. Thus, progressively you can work towards a form that you like.

swift whispy golden

leaf twists brightly like a flame

in the dark river

In class this can be done using an interactive whiteboard, and each selection can be discussed – 'Why is the leaf "swift"? Shall we keep that word or whiz for another one?' – the kind of talk that helps verbal and stylistic discrimination and develops students' ability to edit their own work.

Title Whiz

The inspiration for Title Whiz was the strong set of word patterns found in book titles. Some authors exploit this feature; they use the same formula for each new book and endeavour to make a particular pattern their own. The Harry Potter books come to mind, but there are countless other examples.

To create the Title Whiz, almost 20,000 fantasy and thriller titles and over 8000 from children's books were collected, sifted and sorted, isolating the most common patterns. The classic three-word title ('The' followed by a qualifying word and a main word) proved to be most frequent, and other forms are often variations on this. Other patterns were interesting, although for simplicity's sake they were not included. The three-word pattern is so strong that is perfectly possible to create titles that 'work' by a random process. Bizarre combinations that can be used to stimulate and encourage imaginative work occur, especially if the class is built up to the task step by step.

There are three very extensive word lists to play with, covering children's book titles, fantasy book titles and thriller titles:

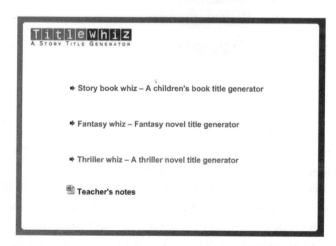

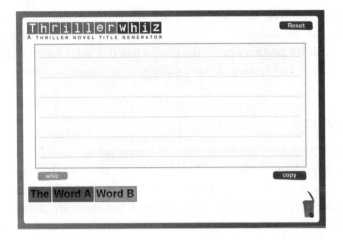

If we arrange the tiles in four rows, we can explore all the permutations simultaneously. Word A performs like an adjective and cannot be used on its own. We can try two forms without the article:

- The, Word A, Word B
- Word A, Word B
- The, Word B
- Word B

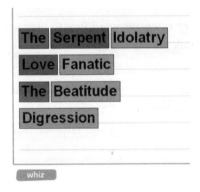

The outcome is the ideal ICT lesson – minimal (but very clever) ICT input with maximum engagement and inspiration from pupils.

The programme will generate a random title each time you click Whiz.

Clicking copy, adds a copy of the current title to the clipboard. When you've finished, simply go into a word processor and select paste and all the titles you've copied in the session will be up on screen. To speed things up, you can create more than one title at a time, as shown. This will give you multiple titles to choose from each time.

1. Drag tiles onto screen.
2. Arrange tiles as shown. Click Whiz.
3. Click copy.
4. Click Whiz as many times as you choose.
5. Click copy to keep a record of the whiz. Paste the results into Word.
6. Click edit to return to the arranging screen.

If you like part of a title, click on the relevant tiles to 'freeze' the words and then Whiz again. Everything except the frozen tiles will spin.

How would you use the results in class? Here's a suggested lesson.

Try this: Imagining a story – a short-burst fiction-workout!

Work in pairs or threes.

Activity 1

Imagine you were going to write a fantasy novel or a thriller – what sort of title would you give it? Write down three ideas.

Activity 2

The computer generates random novel titles. These are created from hundreds of genuine titles 'spun' by the program. Sometimes they make sense – occasionally they don't. Just imagine it's a real, never-seen-before novel. Compare your made-up titles to the computer's random ones. Now choose one title from the computer.

What sort of story do you think it is?

1. What's the main subject?
2. Mystery, fantasy, science fiction, crime, love, espionage?
3. What's the mood? Funny? Romantic? Exciting? Sad?

Activity 3

Imagined details

As a group work on these questions:

What is the main character's name?
Where is it set? Country? City?
Is there a villain? Name?
What happens? Is there some crisis to overcome?
How does the story *end?*
Write the first sentence.

Now get ready to share your ideas with the rest of the class.

Activity 4

Write your own

If you feel really inspired by the story that has come to mind, why not have a go at writing it! There's nothing to stop you!

This sequence builds steadily towards the writing task. It has proved extremely effective – partly because of the collaborative story-construction stage, which links in to children's games and is nearly always highly stimulating. Expect bright shining eyes and excited, enthusiastic minds.

In summary, if we use a computer judiciously we can kick-start an imaginative process that leads to genuine inspiration, motivating students to write because the story that they have mentally constructed is so compelling it cannot be left unwritten! But as always, it's the enthusiasm and drive of the teacher, and the way that a strong collaborative structure is maintained in the classroom that will determine the success of the lesson. A crucial moment will be the feedback session – and judiciously applied encouragement and enthusiasm for the students' prototype narratives can make all the difference.

Does the task outlined here meet the 'inspiration' test? Is the ICT as magically essential as I've claimed? Could the same result be achieved with a dice and bits of paper?

The only real way for you to discover the answers to these questions is not just to read and nod, or shake your head at this book, but to experiment yourself. You will very rapidly find out if using random or dice effects will help some of your students with school-induced writer's block and whether this particular use of ICT suits your practice.

Give it a whirl – or should I say, give it a whizz!

9

Using ICT to Entertain

Every teacher hopes that children will enjoy English lessons and each of us realizes that we need at times to take on the role of entertainer. For many students the varied activities of English are enjoyable, with discussions and debates, stories, language games and plenty of social interaction. There are, however, times when we must admit we're all in need of entertainment, whether to sweeten some repetitive task or brighten the end of the day. If even Plato said, 'Do not keep children to their studies by compulsion but by play', we can feel justified in using ICT along with other methods to make learning more fun. The accounts of activities in earlier chapters have, we hope, demonstrated a variety of ways in which ICT can engage students, often for periods of intense concentration, in ways that will be enjoyable as well as educational. In this chapter we shall look at a number of applications we can use where entertainment is more explicit. The terrible word 'edutainment' was coined in the 1980s for products 'intended to be educational as well as enjoyable', as the *Oxford English Dictionary* puts it. We shall not be using it again, partly because it implies that education and enjoyment are normally in opposition to each other.

The value of ICT can be particularly seen in:

- activities that make repetitive tasks more interesting and motivating
- games and other software with a scoring and competitive element

- applications with a social element, allowing group work and communication inside and outside the classroom
- the creation of films, audio programmes and web pages in a magazine style

Some very simple applications can make lessons easier for everyone as well as more engaging. A computer clock, with countdown and alarm sounds, is more fun than a traditional wall clock, and doesn't rely on you, as a teacher, watching the time as you attempt to keep your well-regulated lesson on schedule. There are plenty available, including those supplied with interactive whiteboards and a countdown timer that allows you to use music (classics or TV theme tunes) on the ClassTools site that features later in this chapter.

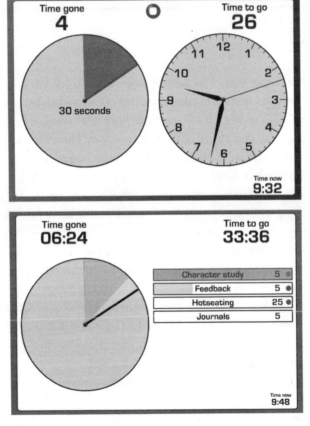

The Teachit Timer makes it easy to set up a sequence of activities

We'd recommend you start by trying the Teachit Timer, illustrated here. This looks good on an interactive whiteboard or just projected on the wall and provides a visual reminder of the remaining time for an activity, complete with a range of fun alarm sounds in additional to a simple gong or bell. Ask students to select the final sound and observe how, when the hand creeps towards the final seconds, group discussion falls quiet as they listen for the bleat of the sheep or the dog's bark. In addition, this timer allows you to set up a sequence of events in advance, so that (if you wish) the whole lesson could be displayed, with visual and audible reminders. The Teachit Timer is free and can be used online or downloaded to your own computer so you can use it anywhere, whether or not you have an internet connection; it's one of the Whizzy Things from Teachit: www.teachit.co.uk.

While you're on the Teachit site, take a look at the many other activities in the Whizzy Things section if you haven't already been tempted to do so by Chapter 8. Most of the interactive resources require you or your institution to take out a subscription but the descriptions and sample activities will give you an indication of what is available and there's even a free version of the Shakespearean Insult Whiz for the iPhone. Designed to work in full screen mode on an interactive whiteboard or classroom screen Whizzy Things can also be used by students on their own or in groups. Anagram and Scramble (making the longest word possible from the given letters, as in the classic television game Countdown) will need no introduction and provide fast-moving activities, with built-in timers, for the beginning or end of a lesson, for example. Magnet is a drag-and-drop equivalent of fridge magnet word games, with considerably more power (including the ability to enter any text, which allows students to add extra 'magnets' and provide multiple words on one 'tile'). You should all be entertained by Weird Whiz, a version of Word Whiz which generates silly sentences to help students to understand sentences and word order. Although the words appear by the random whizzing of the computer, the underlying structure is controlled by dragging the word classes onto the screen, so that 'determiner+adjective+noun+verb+simile' becomes 'the huge gnus boom like bishops at a Beerfest'. We strongly recommend a visit to Teachit to explore for yourself, as the creative minds behind this site (including, we should say, one of the authors of this book) keep adding new activities.

Word games

Word games of various sorts are of course old classroom favourites in one form or another. It is relatively easy to create your own activities such as cloze exercises (where selected words are omitted from the text) using a word processor, though these have limited functionality. An interactive whiteboard offers attractive – and interactive – tools that make it possible to create more tactile games with text, though these take time. Fortunately, there are a number of options for the busy teacher which provide short-cuts to creating your own puzzles or even ready-made activities. Developing Tray, mentioned as a tool for exploring text in Chapter 1, performs this through a deceptively simple activity that can have small groups of students engrossed in discovering a text. This is a commercial program from 2Simple Software (www.2simple.com). Taking its name from the way that, in the days of old-style wet chemistry photography, an image would gradually emerge in the tray of developing liquid, Developing Tray presents students with a hidden text; you can use one of the passages provided or enter text yourself. You can also control how much is revealed to the students at the start. Students then attempt to work out the remaining text by typing letters. They can 'buy' letters – for example to show all the spaces or instances of 'e' – but that will cost points and they soon learn the benefits of attempting to predict letters or even whole words and phrases. While attempting to gain a high score, students will also be interrogating in detail the way the text uses language.

A similar online activity called Revelation was created as part of the Word-Lab from English Online. You (and your students) can sample Revelation at http://bit.ly/te_5. There you will find free versions of some other WordLab games, including the StoryStarter Fruit Machine (described in Chapter 8), Snap, WordSpin and Fridge Magnets. You'll also find Collapser in the Word-Lab; this isn't a game but is worth mentioning here as an invaluable tool for producing collapsed text activities of various kinds: drop any text into the box and the application will turn it into a sorted list at the click of a button. You can then drop the list into a word processor or use them in your interactive whiteboard software. These lists are an excellent way of focusing students' attention on the component words of a text, whether you want to concentrate on the special vocabulary of a poem or the grammatical features of a travel brochure. You could, for example, ask students to sort the text into different categories (they can suggest their own headings). Teachit's Cruncher (available to subscribers) is a similar utility with even more facilities.

Quiz time

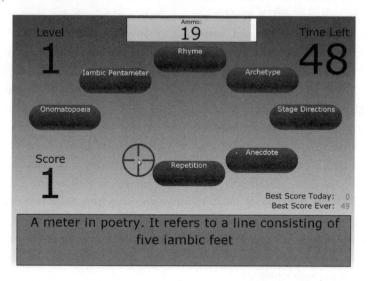

A literary quiz from the ClassTools site

Source: ClassTools from Russel Tarr: classtools.net

English teachers are often, and rightly, sceptical about the kind of software that reduces work to simple right/wrong answers. However, students (especially when preparing for examinations) do need to acquire relevant detail and learn some facts, whether about set texts or spellings, and quick-fire quizzes can be part of the answer. As usual, using a number of strategies gives variety and helps maintain interest. There are several websites which provide tools for you to create your own interactive quizzes. One is ClassTools (www. classtools.net), a free site which includes simple tools which allow you to rapidly create a variety of arcade-type games for students. The same set of questions and answers can be used for several games such as Matching Pairs, Flashcards and Word Shoot (a Space Invaders type of game). It's recommended that questions and answers are typed up as a word processor or text document, in the set format in which the answers are preceded by an asterisk ('What present does Slim give Lennie? *A puppy') – that way, you have the answers to hand as well. Paste this into the online form and select the type of game – it's as simple as that. Furthermore, you can save games to use on your own computer or website if you wish. Because this system is so straightforward and is freely accessible, you can involve students in creating their own quizzes to test each other – always a good way of motivating them.

There are other ways of creating interactive quizzes. One is the suite of programs called Hot Potatoes from the University of Victoria in Canada (http://hotpot.uvic.ca/). It enables you to create multiple-choice, short-answer, jumbled-sentence, crossword, matching, ordering and gap-fill (cloze) exercises for the internet. Unlike ClassTools, which you use online, you need to install Hot Potatoes on a computer (you can download and use it without charge). It's more powerful than ClassTools – it allows you to include text passage and images, for example – and as a result will take a little more time to learn, though there are tutorials and sample activities on the website. In addition, many learning platforms or VLEs such as Moodle have their own built-in quiz creation tools that will be worth exploring. Like Hot Potatoes, these should allow you, if you wish, to use images as well as text and move beyond simple right/wrong answers into more searching tasks (for example, by using multiple choice answers). They could be combined with wikis, online glossaries and questionnaires to introduce or revise aspects of your courses and have the advantage that students in other classes, or later years, can also benefit from these activities.

Try this

This simple way to reinforce key details in a few minutes at the start of the lesson also emphasizes to students that the lesson begins as soon as they come through the door. Create a short PowerPoint presentation providing a few key facts from the last lesson or that you will cover in this session. If you are reading *Of Mice and Men*, for example, this could include aspects of the story so far, such as: 'George and Lennie have come from a town called Weed.' This should be set to run automatically as the class entered the room (using the facility to set up the slide show with a suitably short interval between each slide). Once everyone is settled, stop the presentation and then run a second version in which you control the transition; this time each slide will be a question about the information they have just seen: 'Which town have George and Lennie just left?' and so on. Within a few minutes you've painlessly reviewed the previous lesson and settled the class down. (This idea comes with thanks to Judith Kneen, who first demonstrated it for us.)

The ready availability of video and audio resources online provides another source of material. Sam Custance, teaching 15-year-olds about persuasive techniques in the media, used the archive of television advertisements on the tellyAds site (www.tellyads.com). Her students had a simple persuasive techniques bingo card that she had downloaded from Teachit, with boxes labelled 'emotive pictures', 'rhetorical questions' and so on. As they watched the clips, students completed their cards to see if they could be first to spot all the devices in use. Sam also devised a game to help her students distinguish between fact and opinion and evaluate how information is presented, called 'Who is the biggest slapper?' This required two plastic fly swats, a list of non-fiction and media terminology projected onto her interactive whiteboard and the class divided into two teams, lined up on each side of the board. As she held up different media texts in turn (magazine front covers, film posters, newspaper front pages, etc.) the student at the head of each line used a fly swat to slap the feature they wanted to comment on. The team whose word was hit first went first – if they'd slapped the word 'picture', for example, they had to comment on how the picture was used. Each team had a scribe to jot their ideas down and another student kept the score. Once they had attempted to slap a word with the fly swat and use it correctly, they had to pass the fly swat onto the next member of their team. Sam comments: 'The use of ICT was simplistic – the projection of different sets of words – but it enabled the students to develop their understanding.' This was so successful that she developed the game to include phrases and language devices for the different writing tasks her students faced in the examination and for revising literature texts. Her account of 'Active revision strategies using ICT' is another case study from the NATE project 'Making hard topics easier to teach with ICT' (www.nate.org.uk/htt).

Being sociable

The popularity of networking sites with young people demonstrates how ICT has provided an attractive form of social interaction. We have already learnt in previous chapters how students take to online discussions, sometimes demonstrating far more energy and creativity than they have shown in traditional 'written' work. It is possible to use this to add an extra dimension to classroom study – for example, a teacher asked her class to create Facebook pages for each of the characters in *Pride and Prejudice*. As this was a girls' school, you won't be surprised to learn that Mr Darcy soon collected a large number of friends. If students are enjoying this update on Austen (who has already had plenty of others exploiting her material) they are likely not only to pay closer attention to the text but should also be open to consider the differences between the early nineteenth century and twenty-first century contexts and reflect on their own roles as readers. The use of Facebook in school can be problematic (and it is certainly important that students are made aware of safety and privacy issues online) – in which case a similar activity could be created using a wiki or other facility on the learning platform.

Give them their head

We have already mentioned podcasting in Chapter 3. Even when they were creating study resources many of the students were concerned to present their podcast in ways appropriate to a teenage radio show. This enthusiasm to communicate could be harnessed by encouraging students to create their own magazine programmes or reports on hobbies, interests and other topics of their choice. These could be presented as online publications, audio podcasts or in video format. In the process, of course, students will learn a great deal about media production, audiences and effective communication. Technology allows the results to be shown to the world – or, if preferred, restricted to those with access to the school network or learning platform. Alongside these, or independently, they could run their own discussion forums. Previous chapters have demonstrated how students enjoy being able to debate online; you might like to consider allowing some discussion forums on topics of their own choosing. This will require students to consider who takes responsibility for moderating discussions and what guidelines they will use.

We have now moved away from direct curriculum concerns to wider aspects of communication – but then English has always been about more than examinations and tests. Many of the activities described in this book have appealed to teachers because they offered a fresh approach to teaching and learning but also because they are enjoyable. We know how effective it can be when students bring their own knowledge and enthusiasm to bear on a classroom topic, as was shown in the example described in Chapter 3 of the creation of video game trailers based on *The Strange Case of Dr Jekyll and Mr Hyde*. Chapter 7 shows how reluctant writers were spurred into creativity when given the opportunity to write about what really interested them – manga fiction and video games. Success in each case can be attributed to a combination of the access to suitable tools for the students to express themselves and the teacher's skill in knowing how to encourage them to follow their interests. We hope your students will be similarly inspired.

Glossary

blinds: a feature of software which accompanies most **interactive whiteboards**, allowing 'blinds' to be drawn from the top, bottom or sides of the screen in order to hide parts of the display.

blog: an online journal or diary that allows users to publish material instantly using tools that allow the incorporation of multimedia resources as well as text. Blogger, Typepad and WordPress are examples of popular blogging services.

browser: the software program that displays web pages, such as Mozilla Firefox, Internet Explorer and Safari.

concordance lines: the output of a database used for corpus linguistics. The searched-for word or phrase is typically presented in the middle of a line containing the immediate context; if more context is needed it can be retrieved from the database. Concordance lines provide very useful raw materials for teaching and learning about words.

corpus linguistics: the study of language based on using computers to search large collections of electronically stored texts, analysing the results statistically. A corpus is a collection of texts – several such collections are called corpora.

cropping tool: a tool used in the editing of images, allowing the user to make a smaller image by cropping the top, bottom or sides of a picture.

data projector: a device enabling the display on a computer to be projected onto a wall or screen. It does not require an interactive whiteboard but is often used in conjunction with one.

dialogue box: a window which opens while you are using a program, requesting some input from the user. For example, when Ctrl P is pressed, a 'print' dialogue box opens.

digital camera: a camera that records images in digital format rather than on film; many allow video recording as well as still photography.

digital projector: another term for **data projector** (*qv*).

find and replace: a function of word processors which allows the user to search for a word or phrase and replace it with something different. It can also be used to find and replace a wide range of features such as fonts, highlighting and punctuation.

Google Docs: a web-based word processor, spreadsheet, presentation, form and data storage service offered by Google. This free Web 2.0 service allows users to create and edit documents online, collaborating in real-time with other users; see: docs.google.com

highlight: a tool available in many word processors, enabling text to be emphasized by the use of a digital pen which leaves a mark similar to a coloured highlighter pen.

hyperlink: an area (text or an image) in a document such as a web page which links to another location, either another part of the document or to another document such as a website. Normally clicking on a hyperlink with a mouse takes the user to the new location. Text hyperlinks are usually underlined to identify them, though other conventions such as a contrasting colour are sometimes used.

ICT: information and communication technology: used to indicate the specifically educational applications of technology.

insert comment: a feature of some word processors which enables the user to attach a comment to a specific part of the text. The comment is usually displayed in the margin.

interactive whiteboard: a large interactive display connected to a computer and digital projector. Users can control the display from the computer using a pen, finger or other device on the board.

intranet: a network set up by an organization such as a school for internal use – in other words, unlike the internet, this is normally private.

learning platform: an integrated system to provide information, tools and resources for education, including teaching and learning materials, recording and assessment systems, messaging, wikis, blogs, etc. Also known as a virtual learning environment (VLE) or managed learning environment (MLE), it is usually delivered through a web interface and accessible from both inside and outside the institution. Moodle is an open source example; there are numerous commercial services.

macro: a feature of software programs such as word processors which allow the user to 'record' a series of key presses or mouse clicks. This can be saved so that you can quickly repeat the same process by using a keyboard shortcut.

multimodal/multimodality: a combination of modes of communication, for example, combining graphics, text and audio output with speech, text and touch input.

offline: working with a computer which is not connected to the internet. An offline application does not rely on a connection for it to work.

PDF: portable document format, devised by the Adobe Corporation to allow the creator to share a document with its design fixed. Others can read and print PDF documents but can only edit them with special software. Adobe provides free software, sometimes called the Acrobat reader, which enables users to open PDF documents automatically.

podcast: a portmanteau word combining 'broadcast' and 'iPod' and originally meaning a file (usually audio, sometimes video) stored on a website and then broadcast using a web feed; now used more loosely to describe an audio file found on a website.

right-click: a PC mouse has two buttons – left and right; performing a right-click often brings up an alternative set of choices or a menu.

sort function: a feature of word processors, allowing words or lines to be sorted into alphabetical order.

spotlight: a feature of software which accompanies most interactive whiteboards. Most of the screen is invisible but a movable 'window' of light enables viewers to see and focus on a small area of the whiteboard display.

URL: uniform resource locator – the address used by web **browsers** to locate a resource on the internet, such as www.nate.org.uk.

USB: universal serial bus, a standard for communication between a computer and external devices using a cable; most modern computers have several USB ports that permit the connection of printers, cameras, scanners, USB memory drives ('flash drives', 'pen drives' or 'thumb drives'), etc.

visualizer: a piece of equipment which projects an image from, say, the teacher's desk onto a screen via a data projector. It can be used to show, for example, pupils' work, pictures or text from books or 3D objects. Most will also have a facility to save images.

VLE: virtual learning environment: another term used to describe a **learning platform** (*qv*).

Web 2.0: the generic term for web applications that enable interactive information sharing and collaboration on the World Wide Web. Examples include social networking sites, blogs and wikis, emphasizing peer-to-peer relationships rather than the top-down ones found on static web pages.

wiki: a website that can be edited by users; Wikipedia and Wikispaces are examples: see Chapter 7 for more details.

Further Reading and Browsing

Websites

British Library: access to some of the unrivalled resources of one of the world's great libraries. See especially *Turning the Pages* and the *Learning* section for resources on both language and literature. www.bl.uk

National Association for the Teaching of English: NATE is the UK subject teacher association for all aspects of English from pre-school to university level. There is an area on the NATE site devoted to English and ICT: www.nate.org.uk/ict

National Council of Teachers of English is the equivalent organisation for teachers of English in the United States of America: www.ncte.org

Teachit: an online repository of resources, many free, and interactive materials for subscribers: www. teachit.co.uk. You might like to sign up for the very useful compendium of ideas and techniques delivered once a week for a year – the Teachit Tips service, recommended if you enjoy exploring magic tricks on a computer! http://bit.ly/te_27

Many more useful websites, as well as some additional materials providing detailed guidance on some activities, will be found in the online area for *Teaching English using ICT* on the Continuum site (http://education.rank.continuumbooks.com) and the special area for this book on the authors' own website: www.englishandict.co.uk/te

Books

Tony Archdeacon: *Exciting ICT in English*, Network Educational Press, 2005.

Andrew Goodwyn (ed.): *English in the Digital Age*; information and communications technology and the teaching of English, Cassell, 2000.

Moira Monteith (ed.): *Teaching Secondary School Literacies with ICT*, Open University Press, 2005.

NATE ICT Committee, edited by Trevor Millum and Chris Warren: *Sharing, Not Staring*, NATE 2008; seventeen interactive whiteboard lessons for the English classroom, with CD.

Trevor Millum and Chris Warren: *Twenty Things to do with a Word Processor*, Resource (also available from NATE), 2nd ed. 2005: photocopiable pages with easy-to-use ideas throughout the secondary age range.

Index

Certain terms, such as 'language', 'reading' or 'writing' are not indexed as they permeate the whole book. Readers are also referred to the Glossary on page 163 for definitions of some key technical terms used in the text.